This book is for you if…

- You have been selling relatively simple products or services for a few years and now want to know what it would take to step up to closing 'high value and complex' deals.

- You are already an experienced 'complex sales' professional, but your results are erratic and you are determined to fix that issue.

- You are a Sales Manager or Director whose role requires that you review high value opportunities, decide whether to bid and then coach your team to success.

- You are a Managing Director and want to know what skills and experiences to benchmark a new hire Sales Director or Manager against, or to take part in a Major Deal review.

- You are a Bid Director and want to know how to optimise your relationship with the Sales function through the use of solid processes and procedures.

- You are a Sales oriented Search and Selection professional and you want to know what knowledge and skills to look for in a CV for roles requiring excellence in 'High Value, Complex Deals'.

"Without knowing the force of words, it is impossible to know men."

Confucius

"Nick is the consummate sales professional - he's been there and done it. I can think of no-one better to guide the development of aspiring sales people."

Wojtek Kwiatkowski - VP Sales at a Global Enterprise Software Company

"A motivational and inspiring sales leader who applies his experience, creative thinking and commercial acumen to navigate the complex sales process through to closure. The result - inspired people and over-target performance."

Paul Dickinson - Strategic, Global Tier 1 IT Services & Outsourcing Provider

"Selling complex deals requires determination and stamina. Nick combines these with a very ethical approach which has seen him grow businesses on multiple occasions - Follow him."

Mel Earp - Former Technical Director, Global IT Services Company

"Durable success comes from doing the basics, doing them well and in the correct sequence. Nick's approach gives you the tools to help you get back to those basics, to make them happen well in your business - and turn your actions into success!"

Glenn Taylor - Sales Leader, Supply Chain Transformation, Global Consulting Services Company

"There is nothing training cannot do.
Nothing is above its reach.
It can turn bad morals into good;
it can destroy bad principles and
recreate good ones;
it can lift men to angelship."

Mark Twain

Customers are
F .I. C .K. L .E ™

How to sell large complex deals to equally large and complex clients.

Nick Bailey
MBA, Dip.M, FCIM, FInstSMM

Published by Filament Publishing Ltd
16, Croydon Road, Waddon,
Croydon, Surrey, CR0 4PA UK
Telephone +44 (0)20 8688 2598
Fax +44 (0)20 7183 7186
info@filamentpublishing.com
www.filamentpublishing.com

Printed by Berforts Group - Stevenage and Hastings
Distributed by Gardners

ISBN 978-1-908691-09-5

Nick Bailey

Nick Bailey was born in Crewe, Cheshire, more years ago than he wants to remember. He left school at 16 to join British Telecom (BT) as an apprentice engineer. This was short-lived, so he was soon on the lookout for an alternative career.

Selling had always interested him, so he applied within BT for pre-sales roles configuring and demonstrating PBXs, which he was rejected for on three occasions before he was finally successful.

In 1987, he decided he needed some professional training in bigger systems and applied successfully to Hewlett Packard where he feels he learnt the most in the shortest time about selling computers, solutions and himself. A few years later, he was headhunted by Digital Equipment Corp., where he was exposed to selling services as well as hardware.

He later joined Sema Group (now ATOS) in the early 1990s to sell very large System Integration (SI) deals, followed in later years by Outsourcing (OS). Due to his success in one Outsourcing bid when he beat both IBM and Capgemini, the latter company then put their headhunters onto him and, despite resisting for half a year, he finally moved when the opportunity to develop his career in P&L management came along.

In 2001, he joined Thales Information Systems to do what he knew best in SI and OS Sales. This would turn out to be his most successful period, and he leveraged his hard won experience and skills to lead and grow this organisation from £6m to £60m sales in seven years, complete with a vastly larger Sales team than he had inherited and a string of new high profile clients.

A change in strategy at Thales sadly caused him to think about another move and he joined Invensys IPS as Sales Director for North-West Europe. However, in 2008, the impact of the second largest economic downturn in his career caused him to decide to take a sabbatical in 2009 after 35 years' continuous effort. During the year off, he wrote this book, and the business plan, plus the training courses, for the company that he is now Managing Director of, Apexselling Ltd. The plan was to launch in 2010 but he came to the attention of IBM, a company he had always wanted to work for and still admires today, and so enjoyed a period of time there before giving in to an overwhelming urge to finally run his own show.

Today, he still lives in his beloved Cheshire and is married to his wife of 30 years. They have two difficult to manage teenage daughters, who he adores and wants to get through the university system debt free!

www.apexselling.com

Contents

"Life is either a daring adventure or nothing."

Helen Keller

Foreword

I was both delighted and very honoured when Nick approached me to write this foreword for his new book. It has been a privilege to work alongside Nick on some big deals in my role as Senior Bid Director and to develop a true friendship with him over the past 17 years.

We met in 1995 when Nick completed an internal promotion within what was then Sema Group (now Atos) and he came to work alongside me as the Sales Director for the Manufacturing Sector in IT Outsourcing.

Watching how he worked and led teams was very insightful as he quickly built rapport and support from everyone he worked with. However, what impressed me most was his sheer tenacity and creativity and his support for me in my demanding role with, as is often the case, very limited resources.

Lots of Sales people like to do the customer facing role but when it comes down to being creative, maintaining integrity and working ridiculously long hours with the bid team, they fail the mark.

My abiding memory of Nick is when we worked on a large outsourcing deal together and, because of the demanding timeline for submission and lack of resources, we had to work through the night to get a quality job done. Not just one night but two consecutive ones. Nick stayed with me as together we crafted the words for the customer proposal, and he got the pizzas in at 4am on both mornings to keep us going! Scenarios like that often create deep and respectful bonds between people and that's exactly what happened with us!

Nick has written this book which highlights a lot of other good books and training companies that he admires. So this is a kind of book of books in which his own creativity has again come to the fore with his overarching methodology F.I.C.K.L.E™ and his unique approach to people via the use of the personality typing tool, the Enneagram.

In my view, using World Class Methods AND Processes is the very essence of what successful professional selling really is all about and I truly doubt if you'll find a better set than those which Nick has encapsulated in his book anywhere else on the market today.

Geoff Bingley
Principal Bid Director
Major international Information Technology Services company
February 2012

Acknowledgements

The author would like to thank the following people for their contribution to this book.

- All the Sales, Bid, Technical, Financial and HR teams I have worked with over the last 25 years with whom I've been successful on numerous occasions.

- All the inspirational training course providers and authors referenced in this book.

- The companies I have worked for and their support of me whilst I worked for them.

- Some particularly influential and supportive people who have provided encouragement, advice or supportive quotes for the book, but in particular Geoff Bingley who must be one of the best Bid Directors in the world of IT services, Peter McNab, my friend and coach who taught me all I know about NLP and the Enneagram, and of course Chris Day of Filament Publishing without whom you wouldn't be reading this!

- Last and not least, my wife of 30 years Sandra (that's how long we've been married, not her age...) and our two teenage daughters, Alexandra and Kimberley, all of whom have tolerated the 'Grizzly Bear in the Study' whilst I hacked this out!

"You can preach a better sermon with your life than with your lips."

Oliver Goldsmith

Introduction

Thank you first of all for taking the time to pick up this book and consider buying it. If you've already bought it, or been given it as a present, I believe you are now on the way to becoming, or at least enhancing, your existing abilities to be a 'World Class' salesperson. I use the phrase salesperson deliberately because that's what this book is all about, selling large high value complex deals. Its Unique Selling Proposition (USP) as a book is that, for the first time to my knowledge, it uses the Enneagram, a leading edge personality typing tool, to understand the psychological profile of each of the buyers you face within the context of large complex deal and demonstrates how to use those insights to improve all client facing communication, thereby giving you a competitive edge in future deals. Understanding this is crucial at all of the levels that you may sell at, but even more so at what is known as 'C Level' i.e. CEO, CFO, COO etc, where the time you are given to make and leverage good first impressions is very small and can make or break a deal from the outset of qualification. This book also provides a brand new overarching methodology which is primarily written to help you Find, Investigate, Close, Keep, Leverage and Expand business with clients, hence the mnemonic 'F.I.C.K.L.E'™.

The content also draws on my own 25 year continuous sales experience, ranging from being a junior account manager with Hewlett Packard in the 1980s, to running a pan-European Sales team as a Sales Director for Invensys Process Systems (a division of a FTSE 100 Plc) in 2008, to then finally working in corporate life as an Associate Partner for IBM. In addition, during my career I've worked for Sema Group (now ATOS), Capgemini and Thales Information Systems at Business Unit Sales Director level amongst a few other very small assignments.

Although it draws on my experience in the IT market, the principles are all applicable to other industries where the key need is selling 'high value complex deals'.

Merging all this in-field experience with training received from World Class Sales Training organisations, many of whom are referred to in the text, coupled with the appropriate and relevant academic input from my hard earned 'mature' MBA in Strategic Marketing which I undertook when I was 35, I have integrated this knowledge and experience as concisely and succinctly as possible to appeal to you, the busy Sales Executive. (I know what it feels like not to have the time to read something that just might save me time and make me more money…an interesting paradox) The book not only provides you with a comprehensive, easy to read and easy to follow methodology, it also references what I believe to be some of the 'best-in-class' additional publications and training courses you should also read or attend to augment your knowledge. Some of them are classics in their field and have been around for a while, whilst others are very recent and provide cutting edge thinking.

Finally, if you like what you read here and want to learn more, then please visit my website at www.apexselling.com

The Concept & Method

The concept for this new complex selling model is based on my own developed six step method, which has the mnemonic F.I.C.K.L.E™

Customers, as we know and experience on a daily basis, are very 'fickle' i.e. unpredictable and changeable at any time, so knowing how to sell to them successfully in today's challenging environment is crucial to winning large high value complex deals and ensuring corporate profitability.

F.I.C.K.L.E™ stands for:

Finding – new leads and opportunities
Investigating – prospects issues and ambitions
Closing – getting contracts signed
Keeping – delighting the newly 'won' client
Leveraging – using this success across your customer base
Expanding – winning more work from existing clients

Throughout the F.I.C.K.L.E™ process, we will look at how all communication with clients, whether one to one meetings, presentations or proposals, should take into account 'what kind of people' you are selling to. If you don't accept and adapt to the fact that some of your clients hate minutiae whilst others are turned off by pictures and graphics, then you are automatically and unwittingly introducing competitive disadvantages for yourself.

"If we did the things we are capable of doing, we would literally astound ourselves."

Thomas A Edison

Finding

Stage 1: Finding new leads and opportunities

This stage is really about lead generation, qualification and determining, if the opportunity is interesting, and whether there are any obvious potential differentiators upfront for your product/service.

We are not going to deal with lead generation per se in this book, as it's a wholly separate topic and in fact the responsibility, in my view, of the Marketing Department, not the Sales function. My view may be controversial, but if you are working today for a company with a low investment in marketing and no leads coming in via pro -active campaigns or website, then start to look elsewhere to de-velop your career. Any company that is using its highly paid and qualified Sales force to perform outdated and outmoded activities like 'cold calling' to sell high value complex deals is a 'sunset' company in my view.

Unless you are very lucky and receiving incoming reference based leads, marketing should be correctly using direct, indirect and web based channels to generate leads for you.

To back this thinking up, take a look at David Maister's book *Managing the Professional Service Firm*, where he outlines his views, which I think are also applicable for most types of complex deal led generation, as well as large professional services opportunities. In it, he suggests the following prioritisation, which I've modified and updated very slightly with my own views, for lead generation activity by business development people in such fields:

'The First Team'

- Seminars (small scale)

- Speeches at client industry meetings

- Articles in client oriented (trade) press

- Proprietary research

'The Second String'

- Community/Civic activities e.g. Chambers of Commerce

- Networking with potential referral sources e.g. LinkedIn

- Newsletters

'Clutching at Straws'

- Publicity

- Brochures

- Seminars (ballroom scale)

- Direct Mail

- Cold calls

- Sponsorship (except at Industry events which can work)

- Advertising

- Electronic brochures, DVD, etc

Clearly all of the tools in the last section are successfully used to generate leads for certain categories of products and services, however, the point is that it's unlikely that you will find large complex deals this way. Personally, I would in this era, i.e. the 201Xs, augment the second string category with the Web and the tools it can offer to describe products and services, but more importantly deliver video based customer testimonials, which are extremely important in this category of selling.

Let's assume then that with or without the support of marketing, you have found some useful leads, but what should you do next?

Qualification

Throughout this book, I will refer to many learned publications including books, journals and articles and try, wherever possible, to recognise and credit my sources so that they are references for you to follow up.

In this first instance, however, I am unable to locate the source of the originator of this following mnemonic that I have successfully used in its raw form and enhanced through experience over the last 25 years. It's an excellent tool for initial qualification. My recommendation would be that you take this tool and for each line (and for your particular industry and offering) give each category a points rating and weighting so that when you discuss the outcome with peers and managers, you can 'justify' your thought processes.

It's called the 'S.C.O.T.S.M.A.N', which I have enhanced and transformed with a lifetime of hard won experience with my own "3 R's".

Let's discuss the power of 'Scotsmanrrr'

Solution; Do you have a potential solution to the client's expressed issue or opportunity as they have exactly described it so far? Are you able to articulate both the anticipated quantitative and qualitative potential benefits? Could it, after some in depth consultation, potentially provide the required return on investment (ROI) in the specified timescale?

Competition; What is your competitor's presence in this account? Unless you have significant differentiators, or 'Unique Selling Propositions' (USPs), it's unlikely that you will prevail over an established competitor's relationships and will be merely procurement assessment 'column fodder'. Or worse, be used by savvy buyers to extract a price from to beat down the existing and already favoured suppliers pricing…

Originality; We have previously mentioned USPs and you need to have them. Jack Welch, the famous former CEO of GE, had 'Six Rules' for success. Rule No. 5 is 'If you don't have a competitive advantage, don't compete…' How many times have you bid for an opportunity for reasons other than you have known and demonstrable USPs, e.g. you like the client company or your contacts in it, only to find out downstream that funnily enough those criteria weren't on your client's own buying list…

Timescale; Just how urgent is your client's need? Without time pressure, you are missing one of the most important and 'compelling reasons' why a prospect will spend money with anyone, never mind you. Unless they can give you an absolute 'drop dead' date by when they will have to make a decision, then you need to switch the 'yellow lights' on. I'm sure you know what a yellow light is in a driving context, but for an in-depth explanation, take a look at a sales version of the idea in Mahan Khalsa's excellent book; *Let's Get Real or Let's Not Play*. I have run sales cycles running from 20 minutes, start to finish, to sell a 'small business' PC system to a Glass Manufacturer in Birmingham, UK, (I was focused… it was after all 4.30pm on a Friday afternoon), to the much bigger example of a three year campaign to sell a £17m system integration deal into London Underground (Metro). Sometimes, long sales cycles are justified, but you still have to have a drop dead date and the client needs to be willing to explain to you why they are committed to it.

Size; Size is important regarding your potential results. No doubt you are on a target or quota of some sort and if you are being managed and coached properly, someone like your boss will be sitting with you regularly to challenge you and ask; 'If you have an industry average closure rate of one in three deals, how many deals of what size, in what timeframe, do you need to win in order to make your number, earn your commission and have the privilege of doing it again next year?' Answering this will give you some insight as to whether the deal is worth chasing from you and your employer's point of view. Clearly, in some cases you might want to penetrate a new account just to get a footprint in there, so you could classify something small as 'strategic', but it has to be worth it in the long haul and crucially your management need to be bought in and backing you. Don't take the risk of not having this last piece of support. If you can't get the internal backing, walk away. Remember the very best sales performers walk away from more deals than they pursue at this stage, hence their hit rate is higher.

Money; If you are going to take the trouble to properly rank and weight these criteria, as strongly recommended above, then this is the one item which you must put a heavy emphasis on. Unless the client has a defined budget and you have qualified that fact at CXO level (or in consultation with them, you can generate a Value Proposition (VP) with a Return on Investment (ROI) that will manifest one), then stop now. You are not in the business of writing free specification documents for buyers. The only other justification for continuing is if they let you meet the person responsible for generating their internal business case and they share it with you to the extent that you know your offering will generate their required future ROI. So the options are either they have a budget, will tell you what it is but don't want to share the business case with you at this stage, or they haven't decided the budget yet, but you have enough detail about the business case to know you will be competitive with your anticipated pricing.

Authority; Who is going sign or sanction the Purchase Order (P.O) or cheque and what is the process for its production? We will come on to the importance of knowing who is in the 'Decision Making Unit' (DMU) at a later stage, but even at this early juncture you need to ask the question 'Who signs this off at CXO (Chief - whatever X- Officer) e.g. CFO Level and can we meet them with one of our own Board members please?' If you get resistance from lower buying levels (it's best if you never start there, but we will come onto that later) at this point, you need to seriously consider tactics that will get you higher level access to further qualify the deal, such as asking one of your CXO's to write to whoever is their Executive Sponsor of this project to ask for an introductory meeting. A good justification that normally works is explaining that your anticipated bid costs are considerable and whether to bid at all for this opportunity will be a Board Level decision in your own company. Therefore 'peer to peer' understanding between bidders and buyers is a required process before such funds will be released. If you still get pushback, you can safely walk away because you have just found out you are 'column fodder' i.e. you are not in pole position for this deal in the client's eyes and you are merely making up the evaluation numbers to meet their internal purchasing process requirements.

Need; Again, a very important criteria. An awful lot of companies issue Requests For Proposals/Information (RFP/RFI) without having fully fleshed out the business case (Most top performing sales stars I know never reply to unsolicited 'cold' RFI/Ps on the basis that if they haven't heard about it prior to issuance, written it or influenced it, they can't win it…). It might be however that there is an opportunity to help the client to write or improve it, which is a good way of getting in-depth knowledge of their company, its DMU and re-qualifying all the previous criteria. Let's be clear, in this day and age, no client CXO anywhere will be signing up to something that they can't justify in a Board meeting and ultimately demonstrate business performance improvement. So, similarly, you shouldn't be risking your companies' resources, or your job…, bidding for fantasy ideas generated by middle managers coming up with 'concepts' which don't have a chance of flying with their own bosses (Sorry if this sounds a bit tough, but I've had my time wasted on too many times on this scenario for me not to point it up to you now in order for you to avoid). Work with the client, at 'CXO' Level if possible, to understand what are the demonstrable quantitative and qualitative benefits of this opportunity and why will it be better for their Board to spend their money on this rather than alternative projects competing for the same pot of money.

The 3 R's ...

As stated above, 'Scotsman' is a great start to opportunity qualification and if you thoroughly utilise those criteria alone, you will inevitably increase your 'hit rate' of deal closures. However, my experience over many years and too many deals to count has taught me that you should consider at least three additional criteria at this stage which will inform you even more precisely, and these are what I call the '3 Rs'.

Risk

Relationships

Record

In the 'Investigating' phase discussed in the next chapter, I will share a set of 12 buying criteria that a client project director of one of the world's largest pharmaceutical companies shared with me many years ago. The reason I mention this now is to flag up that despite what you may believe, 'price' is rarely the leading decision criteria in large complex deals...

Be aware from the outset that 'Selling Qualification Criteria' and 'Buyers Selection Criteria' can differ subtly, albeit hopefully, with significant overlap.

These buying criteria helped me to develop the 3 R's.

Understanding the type of products/services being sold by the client's own companies will help you to predict how much importance you and they will put on Risk, Relationships and Record (i.e. your company's track record historically in initially delivering what you've sold successfully and continued to reliably and consistently do so afterwards).

By example, you could easily imagine that Risk and the solid ability to manage it, comes up high on the agenda of buyers in Aerospace, Nuclear, Oil & Gas and Pharmaceutical markets. In fact, in the example I mentioned above, Risk was No. 7 on the Pharmaceutical buyers list and price No.13…

Let's discuss the 3 R's;

Risk; On many occasions during my career, I have had a deal stall just before closure because the client buying team hadn't done sufficient due diligence on the risks inherent in the project to satisfy its own Board and CXO decision makers. These days, I bring it up for them as early as possible… Forecasting a deal internally in your own sales meetings in good faith, based on client buyers feedback of where you stand, only to find out that they themselves hadn't got this crucial area fully covered off and now there is a need for a mere 'few more months' of risk analysis involving third party consultants with a raft of stochastic network tools doesn't go down well back at base.

Understand upfront what risk analysis and management they are expecting from you and make sure you have it. Because you can lose a large complex deal instantly, after months, if not years, of bidding and massive cost, on this one criteria.

Relationships; This is absolutely the most essential criteria of the entire list. Ignore these regularly and you might as well pack up your selling career now. Irrespective of the results of all the formal and informal buying criteria published by the client, the Executive Sponsor of the project you are bidding will buy from the company he or she **TRUSTS THE MOST.** If this is a new opportunity you are working on and you have no relationships, you have to get the prospect to convince you to bid. If they can't explain why it's going to be worth you bidding, stop now and walk away. If you are bidding into an existing client, you must know what they think and feel about you and your company. If you have had a bad project with them in the recent past, don't bother bidding unless you have put it right to their complete satisfaction and more. Think about it like this; If you have ever made a big nerve twitching purchase like giving significant money to a builder to extend your house and it goes wrong, are you going to buy from or recommend that company again? If they put it right and throw in some extras as an apology, does that change your view? That's what it's like for a CXO level person to make a big purchase decision favourably to you or not.

Record; I alluded to this criteria at the end of the last statement. Track record is key, it's the hardest thing to win and the easiest to lose. It's essentially your brand reputation. It costs a small fortune to bid into a new client as compared to taking extension business in an existing one, so don't let whoever delivers your products and services mess it up. Take a follow on interest, without interfering, unless warranted, in the delivery of your company's offerings. Create case studies of success at every opportunity, both internal to the client and for your own external promotional purposes. As a criteria, track record in an existing client is something you must leverage but also compare against other incumbent suppliers.

"Man's mind stretched to a new idea never goes back to its original dimensions."

Oliver Wendell Holmes

Investigating

Stage 2: Investigating the client's issues and ambitions

There are at least three key elements and hence questions to ask yourself about the investigating stage which are;

1. What is the client company about, and what specific problems and opportunities does it face in its own business that might represent downstream opportunities for your products and services?

2. Who are the people in the Decision Making Unit (DMU) that have these problems and opportunities, and what kinds of personalities (types) with what motivations are they?

3. If there are opportunities for you, how are you going to express the benefits of them in quantitative and qualitative terms, such that the USPs of your product or service stand out against the competition (both internal and external) for the budget available?

These questions are being tackled right now by World Class sales teams around the globe in many hundreds of opportunity reviews. Like me, they will have benefited from reading, or being trained by, one or more of the people or organisations who wrote what I class to be the all-time classics of professional complex deal selling. In addition to the book previously mentioned by Mahan Khalsa, *Let's Get Real or Let's Not Play*, the other great books which I strongly recommend to you that I own and leverage in this tome and will reference properly in the appendices are:

- *The Strategic Selling: The Unique Sales System Proven Successful by the America's Best Companies* by Robert B. Miller and Stephen E. Heiman.

- *The New Solution Selling: The Revolutionary Sales Process That is Changing the Way People Sell* by Keith M. Eades.

- *Mastering the Complex Sale: How to Compete and Win When the Stakes are High!* by Jeff Thull.

- *Crossing the Chasm: Marketing and Selling Technology Products to Mainstream Customers* by Geoffrey A. Moore.

- *Consultative Selling: The Hanan Formula for High-Margin Sales at High Levels* by Mack Hanan.

- *Competitive Advantage* by Michael E. Porter.

- *Selling to the Top: David Peoples' Executive Selling Skills* by David A. Peoples.

- *Selling with NLP: Revolutionary New Techniques That Will Double Your Sales Volumes* by Kerry L. Johnson.

- *Managing the Professional Services Firm* by David H. Maister.

- *Killer Presentations: Power to the Imagination to Visualise Your Point - with PowerPoint* by Nicholas B. Oulton.

- *The Wisdom of the Enneagram: Complete Guide to Psychological and Spiritual Growth for the Nine Personality Types* by Don Richard Riso and R. Hudson.

As I mentioned in my introduction, whilst these great books deal with certain aspects of the sales cycle or the types of people you will meet in them, no one, to my knowledge has integrated the whole sales cycle and everything you need to consider, including the critical activity of understanding the psychological profiles of your multi client types, in one book that covers the spectrum from 'Finding' to 'Expanding' and everything in between. This is the USP I offer you in reading this book.

Let's now move to stage one of Investigating, which is to understand the company you have targeted and the problems it faces to the degree that you can confidently perform a secondary opportunity qualification and consider putting this deal in your reported sales funnel with some sort of sensible rating of probability.

Understanding the Company

When I started out in the mid 1980s in the IT sales profession, there was no such thing as the Internet! What this meant was, it was infinitely more difficult to do research on companies and therefore I and other colleagues would spend literally hours writing off requests to get hardcopy Annual Reports, going to libraries and persuading our managers to buy expensive research reports, just to understand the organisations we wanted to sell to. Nowadays, most of this material is publicly available on the Web and thus most stock market savvy prospects and potential clients publish everything you need to know about them and their senior officers for free. So take the time to investigate this, even if you are selling to a midsize company, or even a small start-up. They will almost certainly have enough information on their website to enable you to create a rapport building first client meeting.

The basic initial information you need is;

- Size/turnover of company in whatever currency it reports in?

- Is it growing or slowing, compared to previous years?

- Is it profitable?

- What are their products and services?

- What position in their own market do they hold?

- What opportunities has it expanded into?

- What challenges has it had to face?

- Who is on the organisation chart, and what significant changes of personnel have occurred recently?

- Is any other organisation targeting them as an acquisition?

Once you have this 'profile' in the back of your mind, you are now empowered with the initial data to have an opening conversation with any level of manager, director or VP to further explore specific opportunities. To obtain a more in-depth understanding, you need to build a model and populate it with data along the lines of the 'Ecosystem of Insight' I developed as a young hardware salesman, which is discussed in detail in the 'Expanding' section later.

Understanding the Opportunity

In order to properly understand a client's problems or opportunities, described in some books as 'pain/gain', then it is essential, that as a sales professional, you act in a 'consultative' mode. To get this point across here is another metaphor like the one regarding builders I used earlier. Say you were feeling ill to the point where you needed to go to the doctors. So you go to your GP with a frozen shoulder that you injured at the gym and as soon as you walk in, and after exchanging the usual pleasantries and some light preliminary investigation, the GP says 'I have this great new antibiotic that I think will solve all your problems.' Mmmm, you think, I am not sure sufficient diagnosis has gone on here for him or her to suggest that specific treatment and what's more I am feeling sufficiently uncomfortable that I ignore the suggestion even though I have been seeing this person for many years. What went wrong? The GP made the mistake of prescribing a solution a long way before diagnosing your issue properly. This is exactly what happens with prospects when you see them for the first time and you hit them with all your carefully crafted material about the features and benefits of your products/services based on your own 'second guessing' or anticipation of their issues and needs. Never, ever do this. In fact, try really hard to do exactly the opposite. Imagine yourself as the most conscientious GP with all the time and budget in the world to spend and use your ears and mouth in the ratios they were designed for; 66.6% (two ears) listening and 33.3% (one mouth) probing with questions.

So what questions should you ask at this stage?

Basically, you are trying to establish in quantitative (monetary) and qualitative (i.e. non-monetary terms, say quality, legal, regulatory etc) terms what opportunities and challenges does the prospect face and the degree of importance they have, preferably at Board Level, versus other projects in the business and what is their potential ROI.

In order to get to these, you need an initial overall picture of how the business works from a holistic perspective. To do this is not easy, but I have developed and used one tool based on an approach in Michael Porter's book *Competitive Advantage*, which helps enormously. This is the 'Value Chain' analysis. At its highest level, it is a framework that you can populate on a tailored basis to understand:

- The individual functions in a business

- Where the pain/gain points might be

- What inter-relationships these might have with other functions

- The organisational structure of the company and the owners of the power in it

The approach is again discussed in more depth in the 'Keeping' section later.

Once you have identified and documented the structures and individuals, you are then in a position to 'drill down' into specific issues and opportunities for each one, and can determine the evidence and impact of each on the business.

What you are looking for here is the idea of 'extreme relevancy', which Jeff Thull coined in his insightful book *Mastering the Complex Sale*. It's a process of understanding a client's needs so thoroughly that you are able to precisely match your product and service to meet them, preferably in a differentiated way.

Mahan Khalsa also has an excellent model in his book, previously mentioned, to help you with the conversation during the 'drill down' into their exact need, which is;

- How do you measure it? (the problem or opportunity)

- What is it now?

- What would you like it to be?

- What's the value of the difference?

- Over time?

If you can get the answers to each of these questions for each of the issues and opportunities the client has, then you are operating consultatively and in the best interests of your client, which they will spot, be impressed by and from here on in, you are building vital trust, rapport and critical insights.

In order to develop a quantitative view and if you feel confident and skilled enough to work without a accompanying management consultant, (which you should be to some extent at this level of selling) then take a look at chapter five of Mack Hanan's all-time classic book *Consultative Selling*. The whole book is superb and has kept me in good stead since he trained me and other colleagues in Hewlett Packard as we started our careers there in 1987. It will help you work out which additional questions you might want to use to augment the other processes described previously.

Essentially, the objective is that you gather data to build a business case, based on a clear Value Proposition (VP) which of itself articulates the Return On Investment (ROI) for the client which is ultimately so sufficiently compelling that they are prepared to spend the money with you.

A simplistic example is given on the following page for illustrative purposes based on real case studies from the Pharmaceutical market.

SIMPLE HYPOTHETICAL BUSINESS CASE

INDUSTRY SECTOR   Pharmaceuticals.

CLIENT NEED   Computer Aided New Drug Applications (CANDA).

COMPELLING EVENT   Deadline issued by FDA – all new submissions to be electronic.

BUSINESS BENEFITS   Early introduction of new drug to market, quicker certification.

IT SYSTEM INVESTMENT   Hardware £5m, software £10m, consultancy £12m = £27m.

SCENARIO
1. Normally drug approval cycle is at least 6 years long.
2. New IT system can allow FDA fast search and retrieval taking 1 year off approval cycle.
3. Anticipated new drug sales are £250m/yr.

Therefore business case is:

QUALITATIVE
1. Drug company beats competition to market by 1 year.
2. Acquires FDA approval for new process and submissions

QUANTITATIVE
1. Payback period is £250m ÷ 365 = £700k/day, £27m – S/D = 39 days (i.e. the system pays for itself in 39 days).
2. Return on investment is 1 year additional sales (£250m) - £27m = £223m or 925%

Strictly speaking you should use Net Profit, not Sales, if you can.

Understanding who is involved

Having met your initial contact who is likely to be a middle manager, (its preferable that you start at CXO level somewhere, but these folks tend to delegate the initial vendor contact) you need to leverage your initial rapport with this person to determine all and I mean all, of the people who could have any kind of influence on this project. In one £17m complex deal that I personally sold in 2003, I identified some 39 people I had to meet or present to. This was because the deal was a major software development going into a consortium owned business, which itself was licensed by a transport authority that reported to the Government! The deal took three years to identify and close, and required leading a bid team comprising of a large number of senior and talented individuals without whom it wouldn't have happened. So having made the point, how do you go about finding out who these people are and what to say to them?

Even though it was originally written decades ago, the classic reference on how to start this process is Miller & Heiman's book *Strategic Selling.* I have used their methodology and augmented it significantly with my ideas for the past twenty plus years. It articulates how to think about where you are in the sales process, what 'types' of buyers there might be and what their motivations (or 'personal wins') could be to buy from you. Ultimately, if you follow their method to the end, you will have a permanently developing and dynamic set of actions to move your deal forward.

What they don't cover, as far as I am aware however, is how to recognise what 'personality types' each of the buyers are and how to tailor your organisation's messaging such that you have maximum impact for that individual and their personal interests. The three primer books I would recommend to understand just how important these aspects can be are:

- *The Wisdom of the Enneagram: Complete Guide to Psychological and Spiritual Growth for Nine Personality Types* by Don Richard Riso & R. Hudson.

- *The Personality Compass: A new Way to Understand People* by Diane Turner and Thelma Greco.

- *Selling with NLP: Revolutionary New Techniques That Will Double Your Sales Volumes* by Kerry L. Johnson.

To introduce this section, I am going to also refer to a very simple but stunningly effective story in David Peoples' book *Selling to the Top*, which explains 'Why people buy?'

In it, he cites the ancient philosopher Aristotle and his original theories discussed in his own famous tome 'Rhetoric' and explains why people 'justify on facts' but 'buy on feelings'. This is a crucially important concept to understand if you are to become a World Class salesperson. Clients and prospects will have all the formal criteria in the world but if they really want a particular vendor to win, because they trust them more, then they will.

He goes on talk about why and what 'process' a prospect's mind goes through when they buy, for example, a Porsche, Omega

Watch, Amex Card or dines in an exclusive steak house, when for example the same meal is available at the same quality, but much cheaper, in a franchised outlet within a few hundred metres away! The important point is that none of it is logical decision making. Whilst you could argue that this is Business to Consumer (B2C) buying behaviour, my own experience would say it holds true for a Business to Business (B2B) deal with equal significance.

All of our brains (including yours and the prospect's) run with three processes, which constantly banter with each other until they come to any decision which are;

- LOGOS; what's the logic in this decision? (formal criteria).

- PATHOS; how does this vendor make me feel (emotions) about their solution? (see Miller & Heiman's 'Personal Win' theories).

- ETHOS; can I trust these people once I commit to spending a large amount of money with them? ('I can get fired or promoted on this call/decision'… is the question they will ask themselves …).

My experience would say that the relative weightings you should put on these are that ETHOS are more important than PATHOS, which are more important than LOGOS.

So here is the 'wake up and smell the coffee' enlightenment message.

In big complex expensive long sales cycle deals, having the 'best mousetrap in the world' (functions/features etc) is not necessarily any guarantee of success. It could be much more crucial to have a trusting relationship with all of the CXO members on the evaluation panel.

So how do we get this trust? How do we determine what kind of personalities these people are? And how should we tailor our messaging and communications to optimise our chances?

Knowing what personalities you are selling to

Did you know that the current received thinking as described by Riso and Hudson in their book *The Wisdom of the Ennegram* suggests that there are nine different personality types? If you imagine just how many different buyer roles you will face e.g. Finance, Production, HR, IT etc and then layer into that knowledge the complexity of what kind of person they might be psychologically, this then shows what level of interpersonal communication mastery you need to demonstrate to conclude complex deals successfully.

But how do you even start to get clues to someone's personality when it may be your very first meeting with them?

This is where we will now look at three psychological concepts at a very high level (you can read more in the book list suggested) to enhance:

1.   How to build rapport quickly.

2.   How to use that rapport to help start to define personality type.

3.   How to use your knowledge of personality type to tailor and optimise your communication both verbal and written.

Since 1999, I have been extremely fortunate to work with Peter McNab of www.Excellenceforall.co.uk and now be able to call him my close friend. Peter is one of Europe's (if not, the world's) leading exponents of a self development methodology called Neuro Linguistic Programming (NLP), which many of you will have heard of and the Enneagram (for which he sits on the World Council), and other life enhancing tools and techniques. No doubt many of you will have already been on an NLP course if you are in this profession and have chosen to buy a book like this. For many years, Peter has worked with the UK subsidiaries of Blue Chip organisations, Government and the Big 5 consultancy groups as they were known, before absorption into other entities. I completed my own Certificate and Masters in NLP with Peter and have also had extensive Enneagram training, based on Riso and Hudsons' principles with him. To this day, I am still called back to participate as a volunteer and 'sharpen my saw', as Stephen Covey would say and, to contribute as a Enneagram 'No. 8' type personality in his workshops.

Most of the remainder of this section is based on my interpretation of that training in the big deal context.

Creating Rapport to obtain mutually positive outcomes

The dictionary definition of rapport is;

'relation, connection, sympathy, emotional bond, spiritualistic touch…'

Personally I would swap, in a business context anyway, sympathy for empathy. Emotional bond is still valid and spiritualistic touch, I guess, should be for times with your religious mentor if you have one.

For me, 'business rapport' is typified by a trusting open relationship where a candid and honest exchange of views can take place to explore mutually interesting outcomes.

Taking you back to the house building metaphor earlier, I would hope that you now agree that the followings '4 Cs' represent what any vendor representative needs to create or use to establish sufficient rapport to get a professional dialogue moving. They are;

Credibility; are you dependable and reliable? Do you represent a financially viable company? Do your products and services have a great reputation and consistently deliver on their promises?

Competency; even if all the above is true, are you and your organisation capable of deploying any future solution in this particular client environment, and do you have the references to back it up?

Candidness; are you honest enough and have sufficient integrity, to walk away from the client's issue, if you know full well at the end of this first discussion you don't have a viable solution to meet their needs?

Concerned; Are you really concerned and interested to solve your client's opportunity or issues to the degree where your objective at the end of the project is to turn it into a glowing external reference and case study?

These are what you have to truly feel before you meet the client because his or her own intuition antenna will be on full alert and, as Mahan Khalsa rightly points out in his book, "intent counts more than technique!"

The Preparation

So let's just check before you knock on this person's door…

1. Have you done your background research on this client and their company?

2. Have you an agreed agenda and timing for the meeting?

3. Have you taken the time to call the person's PA and ask subtle but important details, like what the dress culture of this organisation is?

I'm guessing you have all heard of doing (1) and (2) but 3? What's that all about? Well, people buy from people who are like them and if you want to get a feel for how important matching your clothing and details are to creating rapport, then read books by an entrepreneur who you know never wears a tie and has a deep distrust of people who 'look like suits…' This might not seem fair to occasional formal dress wearers, like me and maybe you, but perceptions do create realities and then feelings, which then influence decisions… Further reading on image management to enhance sales and relationships can be done and these include many niche books on this subject in the market.

The First Meeting

First impressions count, so having sorted your head and attitude out and conscious that you are wearing the right clothing, therefore feeling confident and relaxed, the next step is ensuring that your physical introduction is all that it should be.

The first 30 seconds are incredibly simple to do and even simpler to mess up, which will take you a while to recover from if you do. In writing this piece I am conscious that, if I'm a lucky author, many people around the world may be reading this, so just to point out that these next points refer to the Western European/USA/Antipodean style of introductions and protocol. If you are anywhere else in the world, it's certain to be different e.g. Japan where the exchanging of business cards and bowing at the right times to the right angle are crucial. Do your due diligence on these important cultural subtleties beforehand.

So assuming the client's PA has escorted you into their office, the first thing you need to be doing is 'calibrating'. This is a fancy word for doing something that you've done since birth but probably now unconsciously overlook sometimes, which is really noticing the prospect's body language and mood so that you can effect an empathetic introductory statement.

If possible, your 'going in' mindset should be just like the one that you use to meet an old friend (have that exact image in your mind). As an experienced sales person, I'm not going to suggest to you what words you use next because that's up to you and you alone should be comfortable with them. Whatever you do use should show grace, appropriate gratitude and reciprocation, an important aspect.

For the next stage, I stay very business-like and I ask if it's OK to re -review a previously proposed agenda (which will have an outcome based objective) and the timing to check whether all what was agreed during the making of the appointment is still OK, because often it isn't and you have even less time…

This is now the time to consider some very subtle NLP techniques called 'matching and mirroring'. It's a known fact that if you mirror exactly the posture of your prospect, they will warm to you, except if they are sitting there with their arms folded (How to get these unfolded is best read about in any quality NLP book.). You need to do it subtly…and it doesn't involve a physical interaction!

It's important to know that the use of NLP or the Enneagram is not about 'manipulation'. What we are trying to achieve is the most harmonious interpersonal environment so that both parties maximise the usefulness of the meeting and can move forward productively. Personally I believe both of these methods should be taught in schools. I'm convinced the world would be a happier and more settled place…

So by now, you have calibrated their mood, made your introductions and successfully matched or mirrored their posture, the agenda is set and the clock is ticking.

The next communication model we will utilise to understand how to generate genuine rapport is the Target Model, developed by my coach Peter McNab as graphically represented below;

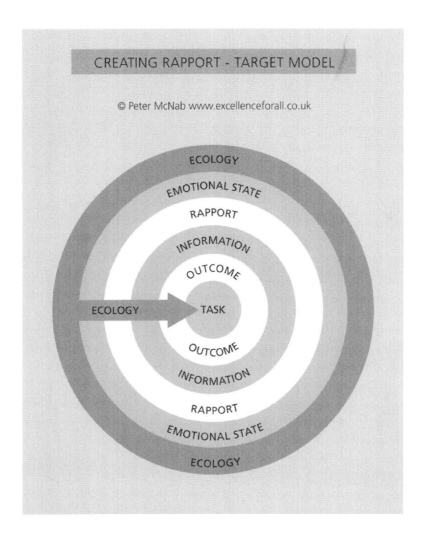

CREATING RAPPORT - TARGET MODEL

© Peter McNab www.excellenceforall.co.uk

ECOLOGY
EMOTIONAL STATE
RAPPORT
INFORMATION
OUTCOME
ECOLOGY → TASK
OUTCOME
INFORMATION
RAPPORT
EMOTIONAL STATE
ECOLOGY

Conceptually in any discussion, the model suggests that you move in stages from the outer ring to the result or task in the middle. The very outer ring talks about ecology, which is ensuring that the discussion is taking place in a sufficiently 'safe' environment. The next ring inwards is the emotional state which you have covered off by calibrating them, the initial and sufficient rapport has been established and now you want to focus on the task in hand, which is to generate enough interest for you to walk out with a qualified lead based on the information gleaned. So Peter's point in the model, and it reflects my earlier comments about GP's diagnosing before prescribing, is not to jump straight to 'task' or outcome discussions or solutions (in fact, Mahan Khalsa has a phrase which is called 'move off the solution'!).

Now is the time to show the concern we mentioned earlier and to ask open 'Socratic' questions about the issues and opportunities your client faces in their business and to discuss them in qualitative and quantitative terms. Make a list of these issues, get agreement they are worth tackling and ask the client to prioritise them for you. Once you have the depth of information required, you can agree on the outcomes of the meeting and next steps, hopefully with a series of actions or tasks associated to follow up on, and an opportunity to maintain deal momentum.

Who else is involved?

Having got the list of issues and understood their potential impact on the business from your initial client contact, the next key step before declaring this information a real opportunity to your company is to find out who else is involved, what degree of interest they have in these issues, what role they will play in this procurement, i.e. 'gatekeeper' and what personality types they are. This last point is very important because from here on in, you will need to tune your communication style to the communication preferences of your message recipients. You may well understand that some people prefer 'pictures' to 'detail' as I do, but there is more depth to investigate in order to be able to affect persuasive messaging in whatever method you use, e.g. proposal, presentation, webinar, etc.

So a key action in your wrap up conversation with your initial contact, if not during the initial discovery phase of discussing their issues and opportunities, is to ask some very direct and searching questions about 'who else is involved?' Depending on the size of the project, it may only require the involvement of a few key people mandated by the Executive Sponsor in order to maintain speed and balance of decision making. Or, it could be many dozens of interested people who have genuine influence because you are selling to a consortium.

One of the very best tool and methodologies available for mapping out the Decision Making Unit (DMU) and has been for many decades is the Miller & Heiman 'Blue Sheet' from their book and course *Strategic Selling*, which I undertook in 1987.

In a heavily modified form, for my own personal use, I utilise this as a documented basis to help me figure out 'who else might be involved?' In the actual 'Blue Sheet', they talk about four different categories of influencers: Economic, Technical, Users and Coach. I used to remember these categories by converting this to the acronym 'C.U.T.E'. In my own version, I use 'C.A.U.S.E.D', as most high value complex deals have in my own experience a minimum of six different types of buyer, and these are:

C hampion, or Coach if you prefer. This person is leading the vendor interactions on behalf of the buying organisations evaluation team and is usually the source of most points of clarification.

A nalyst(s). These can be multiple sets of people whose job is to 'analyse' various aspects of your bid. Due to the complexity, they can typically separately cover technologies, processes, finance, legal, regulatory etc.

U ser(s). These are the people who will actually use your solution, be they engineers, call centre staff, finance experts or whoever. They will judge your solution on how it improves their life qualitatively and quantitatively.

S ponsor. This is typically the Executive level sponsor sitting on the Board of the buying organisation and will recommend or otherwise your solution to their peers at a sign-off meeting.

E conomic. This is always the CFO or Finance Director, and will be separate from the Sponsor but may well be one of the 'Decision Makers' spoken about next. However, this person's role is to measure the Return On Investment (ROI), Payback Period and Breakeven point of your project, versus other capital projects that the company could utilise. Note at this point your offer is not just competing against your direct competitors but entirely different projects competing for the same investment pot…

D ecision Maker(s). This is a definitive list of people across all departments in the business who have to say 'yes' before the Board will sign it off themselves. You need to know every one of these and they may well have dual roles and be one of the above as well. i.e an Analyst.

You will see this range of contacts for you to highlight in my 'Dynamic Contact Plan'.

Miller & Heiman suggest you need to understand what the 'personal wins' these individuals will get from buying your solution are, but also and crucially, in order to differentiate my communications to them, you must try and determine what kind of personality type they are. This is where we now come full circle back to the '9 Types' mentioned previously and categorised by a tool called the Enneagram.

The Enneagram

The Enneagram has been written about by many authors, but in my opinion one of the best books on the subject is *The Wisdom of the Enneagram* by Riso and Hudson. On their website, there is a comprehensive justification as to how and why the Enneagram works so well, and here is in of my favourite extracts;

"Even if we understand that different people need to be managed differently, without an adequate idea of *what those differences actually are*, it is difficult to manage people more effectively. Once type differences are taken into account, however, solutions grow out of insights about the nature of each type, its habitual reactions, and its motivations. When type is taken into account, communication becomes exponentially more effective and people can recognize and make the most of *human diversity*."
(source; www.enneagramlondon.com)

If you substitute the word 'manage' in the above text to 'sell to', then you will understand the significance of this tool in the context of this book.

Once you take the initial analysis test provided in their book for yourself and then start to read about and explore your own type, you would have thought someone had read your mind and felt your heart: it's so accurate!

'FAMOUS' ENNEAGRAM TYPES

TYPE 1 - 'Lecturers' e.g. Gandhi, H Clinton, Nader, Streep, 'Spock'

TYPE 2 - 'Carers' e.g. Confucious, Teresa, Sheen, Alda, 'McCoy'

TYPE 3 - 'Achievers' e.g. B Clinton, Winfrey, Stone, Schwarznegger

TYPE 4 - 'Creators' e.g. Bergman, Simon, Dylan, Jackson, Garland

TYPE 5 - 'Analysers' e.g. Einstein, Hawking, Gates, Fischer, Nietsche

TYPE 6 - 'Accounters' e.g. Bush, Hanks, Springsteen, Gibson, Hoover

TYPE 7 - 'Adventurers' e.g. JFK, Taylor, Spielberg, Williams, Jagger

TYPE 8 - 'Leaders' e.g. FDR, LBJ, Gorbachev, Wayne, Heston, Castro

TYPE 9 - 'Brokers' e.g. Lincoln, Reagan, Jung, Disney, Loren, Costner

For a bit of light relief at this point in the book, take a look at the example of certain famous people and where they might have been on the Enneagream on the previous page.

Understanding yourself and the impact you have on others is a key part of World Class sales performance and I would strongly recommend you partake in this self analysis (even do a course, which would be better, because you can't really feel the impact of this material without interaction with the other eight types you live with on a daily basis). Having acquired some insight into yourself, the next step is to really understand 'where are these other people coming from?' (… the DMU) and of course I don't mean their hometown or city but their psychological make-up and motivations.

Riso and Hudson have developed the generic model used in their book and enhanced it for business use. If you go to their website, it describes the 'business type' names for each of the nine spaces, one of which we all occupy. I provide my own interpretation to use in a sales context later. It's important to know that no one is attempting to put something as complicated and unique as a human being into a 'pigeon-hole', but these tools will get you a lot closer to understanding interpersonal differences, which alone will make a dramatic difference to your communications and results with them. If you have ever had a conversation with someone and in the extreme circumstance afterwards thought how much you didn't like that person and hoped you'd never see them again, or conversely met someone and within hours hoped they'd be your future friend for life, then start investigating the Enneagram. It's a truly insightful, fascinating and ultimately effective tool.

My personal interpretation and basic overview of it is as follows;

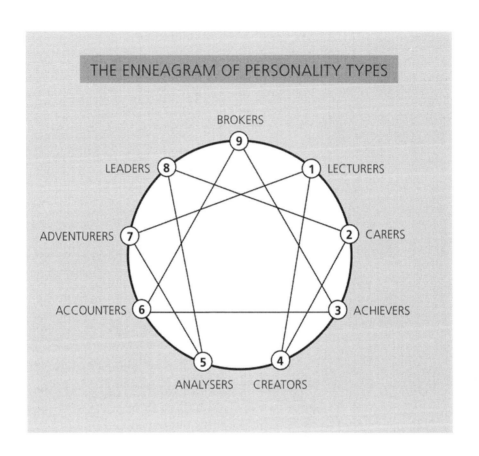

THE ENNEAGRAM OF PERSONALITY TYPES

BROKERS

9

LEADERS 8   1 LECTURERS

ADVENTURERS 7   2 CARERS

ACCOUNTERS 6   3 ACHIEVERS

5   4

ANALYSERS   CREATORS

As mentioned before the theory is that there are nine distinct types of personality. At the high or 'meta' level, spaces 2 - 4 are 'heart' spaces, 5 - 7 are 'head' spaces and 8 - 1 'gut' spaces. This means that for whichever space or number you find yourself in, you will 'primarily' relate to the world and the people in it, from your heart, head or gut. I am an '8' and will always, in the final reckoning of any important decision, run with what my gut is telling me. Also, I put high value on 'Autonomy' whereas other spaces place higher value on 'Security' or 'Attention'. People in the head spaces i.e. 5 - 7 will be irritated by this because to them all decisions should be logically made by lists and details and analysis, all of which can be helpful to me as well, but in the end my 'gut' makes the decision. This can be so powerful for me that when my wife showed me a range of holidays to choose from to celebrate my fiftieth birthday I picked, in two minutes, going to the Maldives to scuba dive with giant manta rays, purely on gut feeling, and just 'knew' that would be right for me.

So what, may you ask, is the importance of all this understanding in selling? Well this is where I start to add deep value from years of experience and integrate for you and your benefit, the various tools and techniques in a symbiotic way, which will give you a real set of competitive advantages in your next big deal.

Whether or not you choose to utilise a proprietary model from a previous training course or knock out a 'contact plan' model that suits you in order to identify 'who is involved' in your complex deal doesn't matter, as long as you have one. I have provided my version for your use here.

DYNAMIC CONTACT PLAN

SCOTSMAN RRR

CLIENT:	DESCRIBE QUALIFICATION OUTCOME	WHERE IN THE SALES CYCLE?	
SECTOR:		F	
OPPORTUNITY:		I	
		C	
VALUE:		K	
CLOSE DATE:		L	
		E	
NAMES OF DMU AND 'TYPE' 1-9	DESCRIBE 'C' LEVEL CONTACT PLAN	DESCRIBE USP'S	
C			
A			
U			
S			
E	DESCRIBE PROJECT CLOSE PLAN	UPDATE ACTION LIST HERE	
D			
DESCRIBE VALUE PROPOSITION			

So the questions are; 'what are my client's motivations and how do I optimise my messaging to them?' In your contact plan, you will need to have;

1.   A list of the people involved and their titles.

2.   A reason these people might want to buy from you.

3.   An idea of their personality type (we will use the above material in a moment to show how this can be done approximately 'on the hoof').

4.   Where they sit in the organisation.

5.   Which of the people involved has the most pain/gain involved with this deal?

6.   The competition and their potential advantages.

Once we have this basic information, we need to know how and when and by who the decision to buy is going to be made. Rather than re-invent the wheel, here is Mahan Khalsa's 'Decision Grid'.

DECISION GRID

From Mahan Khalsa's book 'Let's Get Real or Let's Not Play'

STEPS	DECISION	WHEN	WHO	HOW

© 1999 Franklin Covey Co

Now that you have all the basic information to analyse and progress your deal, you need to rapidly start to gather information by using 'body language' as to their potential type from 1 - 9.

Using the high level model, unless people are 'in the wrong job', their job function and role is the first real clue. From my experience, the head, heart, gut model can now be augmented with role types. This next piece is purely experiential and non-scientific, but has through much practice proved to be a very accurate guide for myself. My take on the Enneagram types by typical job function is;

- '1's are the lecturers, teachers, quality controllers.

- '2's are the carers, nurses, doctors, therapists.

- '3's are the achievers, sales, coaches.

- '4's are the uniques, artists and 'special' people, actors.

- '5's are the analyticals, computer techs, scientists, R&D.

- '6's are the logicals, accountants, methodical, risk averse.

- '7's are the adventurers, risk takers, sales.

- '8's are the entrepreneurs, commanders, leaders, visionaries.

- '9's are the developers, peacemakers, diplomats, brokers.

So let's take one of these types and walk through how you would get a better and more accurate view of them and how to tailor any future piece of communication to them. A person that will be involved in any large complex deal is the Chief Financial Officer (CFO). My experience would suggest that these people will either be a 6, 5 or 1, in that order. The way to further qualify that in dialogue with them is to use body language. One of the better books on body language in a selling situation is *Selling with NLP* by Kerry Johnson if you want to get a deeper understanding. Again, my previous comment holds; books are great, courses are better, but then you need to use and practice it all in the field.

Selling to each 'type'

What follows now is my take on how the Enneagram works for each personality type based on experience, not science, so you need to factor it with your own views. Being able to spot what 'types' your client's DMU is made up of is about acute observation and listening techniques which is a practice and skill you will hone over time.

N.B No one type is any better to be than another…we are what we are…the prize is to get along with them all.

Type 1's are what I call the 'Lecturers'. These people are about correctness and detail; you can imagine them marking papers. In order to influence them, you need to have high quality communication which is concise and to the point, covering all the angles. The clues to recognising them are squeaky clean desks, in control, efficient and micro detail questions.

Type 2's are what I call the 'Carers'. These people are about 'other people' to the extent that they don't understand their own needs and feelings. In order to have rapport with them, you need to be concerned with teamwork. You can recognise them via traits such as 'softly-spoken' and sometimes they can be relatively unassertive, as they hate saying 'no'. They tend to excel in support roles.

Type '3's are the 'Achievers' and in my view most of the best salespeople come from this space. Note I say salespeople, not sales managers or directors. They are very big on acquiring all of the trappings a materially successful life has to offer and they go after them zealously. They are very competitive and hardworking and place value on recognition by others. Some do have a high detail orientation.

They are comparatively easier to sell to as they tend to be very personable and will listen to propositions. On a personal level, these people will buy things that make them look a success, i.e. the latest gadgets, clothes, cars, and can be very up to date with everything.

Type 4's are the 'Creators'. These people place individuality high on the agenda. They see themselves as 'special' and want to be treated as such. There will be one of these in your life somewhere and they can be recognised as the person who makes you feel as though you need to 'walk on eggshells' to avoid upsetting them (although you won't know when you have...). Selling to them can be difficult as they have mood swings and are probably the most 'fickle' of all the types. Appealing to their deep sense of creativity and asking for their unique ideas and contributions is probably the best way.

's are the 'Analysers'. These are the folks you will find in
ke '4's, they can be innovative but more in an engineering
sense than an artistic or creative one. They have no concept of the
importance of time and believe that 'finding stuff out' is more
important than on-time delivery. Selling to them is about exciting
them with something that is 'cutting edge' and contributes to
their knowledge base.

Type '6's are the 'Accounters'. These people are highly risk averse
but also big on team play. These people will want to balance and
understand the 'pros and cons' of any proposition you pitch to
them so that they can come to a logically argued conclusion.
Hence the best way to obtain rapport with these people is to be
equally factual, logical and well judged in your communications
with them and ensure all risks are mitigated.

Type '7's are the 'Adventurers'. After '3's, these make the next
best sales people in my view. Highly upbeat and enthusiastic, they
can often be overly and unrealistically optimistic about situations
(Sales managers, beware). They get bored very easily and will want
to 'move-on' once the big picture has been established. Again, like
'3's, they are relatively easy to relate to as they are high on interpersonal skills and will experiment easily. The key with '7's is to
stay away from boring details and focus on the big goal that
needs to be achieved.

Type '8's are the 'Leaders'. This type want to know what the big
picture is as well as '7's, but additionally they want the 'plan'.
"Plan the work, work the plan" is probably their motto. Their innate
self-confidence and need to be in control means that in order to
relate to them, you need to be clear, assertive and specific. To sell

to them, use pictures, charts and don't hide problems, just say how they can be managed. Be respectful, but certainly not over deferential, which they will interpret as a sign of weakness.

Type '9's are the Brokers; not in a financial sense, but in an inter-personal one. They are very keen on having a harmonious working environment and are the internal 'diplomats' of the company. Clues to them include amiability, concern, waiting for others to speak/contribute. In order to sell to them, your ideas need to cause minimum disruption and serve the greater whole. Any changes proposed need to be seen in a very positive light for as many people as possible to maintain group harmony.

Using body language and NLP techniques, we are now going to look and listen to our contacts to further calibrate their communication preferences. The first thing to observe are eye movements as illustrated next.

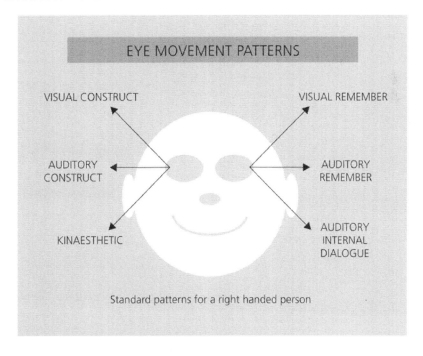

If your contact is continually looking sideways when you ask them a question, then they are either remembering or constructing 'auditory'. If they do this continuously, in preference to accessing their feelings (looking down), or imagining (looking up), then you know they have a strong auditory preference. This orientation was so strong in a CFO I knew (he hired me into Sema Group) that he actually asked me not to show him any presentation graphics, but just 'talk him through' a major issue we were debating, such was his 'auditory' bias. The point about this is that for every person in the DMU that you are selling to, you must tailor your verbal and written communications to them in order to maximise their effect and your influence and not switch their concentration off.

So by example, don't;

1.   Show lots of graphics to 'auditory' CFOs who have a passion for numerical detail and analysis as I did...

2.   Show lots of detail to a visionary entrepreneur (8) who only wants to 'see' (visual) the big picture and, providing his CFO tells him the numbers stack up, will decide to go with you on 'gut feeling'.

3.   Make the mistake of not taking the time to create lots of rapport and interest in the personal lives of anyone you think is in the 2 - 4 spaces, because they are the people 'people'.

At this stage, you may be forgiven for thinking this is too complex, but it isn't really when you've practiced it enough. The key is to break it down into simple steps;

1. What role and likely space type do they have?

2. What language do they use the most? 'See', 'Hear' or 'Feel' language? In other words, are they Visual, Auditory or Kinaesthetic in NLP terms?

3. How do you calibrate their interpersonal style? Do they want to just get on with it, or do they want to chat before they get down to it?

Once you have a broad outline of their preferences, start to tailor your communications style accordingly. For more insights, do yourself a big favour and get a copy of Peter McNab's NLP Practitioner Prompt Cards from www.excellenceforall.co.uk, which is a laminated set of easy to read 'quick reference sheets' you can use in the field and on calls. Better still, attend one of his courses!

Communication and Building Trust

If you have followed my advice so far, in summary you should have the following covered;

1. Have met and attempted to 'type' by Enneagram description each influential member in the Decision Making Unit (DMU) for this deal.

2. Have got an initial feel for what they need from this project to fulfil their business criteria as a supplier.

3. Have secured sufficient quantitative (financial) and qualitative (objectives) information to understand their business case.

4. Using the qualitative data, have an understanding of how to position your offering to reflect your USPs against their needs in a way that differentiates you from the competition.

5. Will be starting to build trust by demonstrating the 4 C's, i.e. Credibility, Competency, Candidness and Concern.

On the assumption that all of this is in place, or soon will be, then it's likely that you will be putting together some form of written proposal followed by a presentation. Few deals of any size or stature get away with not doing both of these at least once.

It's at this point that you need to take stock and have a long and deep brainstorming session with your bid manager and anyone else who is likely to be contributing collateral to the proposal and follow on presentation. Put a whole day at least aside to discuss and agree the following;

1. Consensus on exactly what the client is looking for.

2. How that can be matched to your offer in a way that differentiates you from the competition.

3. Who are the people involved and what messaging do they need to get?

4. Given your view of the DMU participants, what are the dominant Enneagram types and therefore what balance of 'See, Hear, Feel' should be played into the proposal and presentation?

(N.B the 'Feel' types on spaces 2 - 4 will be keen to meet you, your delivery team and your reference customers, so make sure every opportunity to do this is taken up for them in particular.)

In order to maximise the communication tailoring, the ideal position to be in is to know just how the client is likely to evaluate you versus the competition. Going back to a previous chapter where we discussed that ETHOS (Trust) was probably more important than PATHOS (Emotion), which itself was more powerful than LOGOS (Logic), take a look at this buying criteria list for a major software development project, given in priority order, that was made privy to me by a contact in one of the world's largest pharmaceutical companies many years ago;

1.   Understanding the application

2.   Flexibility of interpretation

3.   Financial stability

4.   Accuracy of estimate

5.   Technical experience

6.   Quality system

7.   Risk identification and management

8.   Documentation

9.   Project Planning & Control

10. Location

11. Day Rates

12. Overall Price

If that list doesn't reflect the importance of understanding the 4 C's rather than having best price, I don't know what else will.

Moving on to building the proposal and presentation, there are some key overarching points regarding structure and content to reflect the above, which are;

- You must be able to describe the whole proposal in an Executive Summary (which may form the opening few slides of a larger presentation too) that is no longer than two A4 sides of paper. The structure of the summary should follow the time honoured advertising world's acronym of A.I.D.A, meaning get their Attention first, develop Interest, create deep Desire and close by calling for Action.

- **Attention** is about demonstrating in a very few lines how well you understand your client's issue or opportunity, such that they are saying to themselves; "well these folks really have got to the heart of our requirements here!"

- **Interest** is about showing your concern and where also you show your 'flexibility of interpretation' as described previously, demonstrating that you have weighed up all the known pros and cons, and are making a specific recommendation albeit with a small number of potential tweaks if required.

- Desire is about making the whole deal compelling, in other words you are putting a deal on the table that shows you have taken into account any budgetary, technical or legal constraints the client has and have adapted your offer to suit their circumstances in an innovative way, which further differentiates you from the competition.

- Action is about asking for the order in the subtlest way possible in writing. Here you need to create additional compelling events that augment the business case you have presented but now puts a specific timeframe or other compelling reason on the deal to bring it home sooner rather than later. Always remember the metaphor that you haven't won the motor race until the chequered flag drops on your car first. Letters of Intent and wishful thinking are not bookable devices in your own CFO's eyes.

Once you have this outline deal constructed and articulated, you should ensure for the Executive Summary that it's no more than two A4 sides of paper or five to seven slides.

You now need to flesh out the detail of each component of the deal is sufficient depth and style to match the needs of the individual interests of each member of the DMU. This is because each member, once they understand the Executive Summary, will not read the whole proposal. I'll say it again, **they will not read the whole proposal**…What they will read is the bit that interests them and that they have to sign off to in recommending your solution. So, by example and thinking about the Enneagram types again, the CIO will be looking at the Exec Summary plus the IT component only. They will not be doing their lawyer's job of checking the

Terms and Conditions. So if you think the CIO is a '6' and quite auditory don't bother putting lots of graphical schematics in, just describe the approach and the components and provide the background logic to your recommendations in a factual and unemotional way with no unwanted 'feature superlatives'! In fact, if you have the opportunity, check with them directly exactly what parts of the proposal are most important to them and what are their 'must-sees'.

Now go through each of the DMU types and tailor your words to what you think they want to see, hear and feel about your solution and that accurately reflects its genuine capabilities.

In conclusion, the Executive Summary should try and cater for all the personality types who you know will read the document. The main body, however, should be individually tailored to communicate your technical, legal, political and financial concepts. You must be able to finish the document with a compelling and differentiated rationale as to why they should buy your solution and not the competitions. In fact, you should have those thoughts in your mind all the way through the sales cycle and if at any time you can't articulate it then you should re-qualify the deal formally, instead of wasting bid budget just because the deal has created its own momentum, which is a mistake junior salespeople regularly make...

The Presentation

Regarding presentations that follow on from a proposal and support the bid submission, the main points to consider are;

- The structure should mimic the Executive Summary but should have sufficient detail to satisfy all interested parties and their 'personal' interests, checking with your 'Coach' that you have all the bases covered.

- Each slide should have no more than 5 - 7 points.

- You must, if available, use your strongest customer testimonials and case studies.

- You should finish with a synopsis of how your offering matches the given or confirmed client buying criteria, and ask for acknowledgement from the audience for each one that they agree with you on your compliance.

- Never, ever agree to give the presentation unless ALL members of the DMU attend and most critically, the client's Executive Sponsor of the project. If they will not field these individuals, they are sending you the strongest possible signal that you are just making up the numbers. This is where you should be courageous and refuse to present and just see what happens. If they want you and you are in pole position, then they will make the effort to attend. If not, then don't waste your time and walk away unless they have a very convincing excuse.

Presentations are a whole field of expertise in their own right, but a good primer is Nicholas Oulton's book *Killer Presentations*.

"To win a hundred victories in a hundred battles is not a hallmark of skill.
The acme of skill is to subdue the enemy without even fighting."

Sun Tzu

Closing

Stage 3: Closing the deal

It almost goes without saying that closing the deal is the most important phase of the whole sales cycle. If you don't close deals, you won't have a company for very long, a mute point sometimes lost on non-sales types who look down on the sales profession unwittingly. Until you sell (close) something, there is no need for anyone or anything else (although clearly you have to have something to sell in the first place i.e. a product or service, so again it is a team thing, but they can make as many of them as they like. If they aren't sold, there isn't a business...). Remember though that selling is a team game and there is no 'I' in 'Team'. It's vital you have representatives from all the disciplines appropriate at your presentation including your best technical people as well as commercial. It's stating the obvious, I know, but closing is the phase where most 'average', as opposed to 'high performing', sales people come unstuck. It's also the phase most shrouded in mystique, because people sitting outside of the sales discipline know how important it is and are intrigued about how it's done. I am even willing to bet that seasoned sales people scanning this book in a store wondering whether to buy it will have jumped straight to this chapter to see if they can glean some quick tips or to test the thinking as a qualifier, regarding whether they invest in the book.

Just an aside for a moment, don't make the mistake of believing the so-called current wisdom in some of the latest sales training books regarding closing. In some, but not all, they are now suggesting that deals close themselves, or should do if the upfront work has been done properly (I can hear time-served sales superstars crying with laughter now…). The truth is they don't close themselves and you have to be in total control of this really intensive phase until you have a signed contract.

The reason behind closing becoming difficult is not, however, down to the salesperson in the main. The reason is that this is the stage where the buyers, not the sellers, feel under the most pressure. It's that they are about to commit millions of pounds, dollars, euros or whatever currency, to make a potentially career enhancing, or worse, limiting decision. Because closing is about gaining consensus and getting a decision and an irrevocable one at that. The word decision comes from the ancient times and in a literal sense means 'to cut', meaning no way back, or in a modern commercial sense not without a lot of work or money. Just as you can't 'half decide' to get married or buy a house, you either do or you don't, it's binary, and that's what you must have in your deal commitment from your client. In most countries the accounting laws now prevent you from booking anything less than a formal Purchase Order signed by a Board member or their appointed legal delegate. Your own CFO will not book Letters of Intent (LOI), unsigned emails or faxes…So how do we get to this point with the client?

Again, we go back to some overarching simple structures and processes that can be utilised time after time, which I have developed over the decades.

Project Plan (Closing Plan)

A big deal is really a project and if your bid manager hasn't done it for you in the overall bid, then at this stage you want a detailed project (Gantt/PERT) style plan to cover the period, process and actions between post presentation and closure. It's key that three elements are included in this plan;

1. You must have a plan to cover the client's timings and actions. Let's call it the external plan.

2. Similarly you must have the same for your own internal actions and importantly these two plans absolutely must be synched with dependencies highlighted.

3. Finally you must get the client's plan signed off and agreed to with all the required resources lined up to work with you e.g. lawyers for T&Cs etc.

I have during my career been very privileged to work with some brilliant colleagues from Bids, Legal, Technical, HR and Finance and, without them, could not have won anything. These kind of deals are the biggest 'team sell' you can be involved with. As you might imagine and maybe empathise with, you don't always get the 'A' team, and some of what follows describes how I have had to demonstrate leadership analogous to a 'diplomatic orchestral conductor' for the occasional team member who wasn't as engaged or motivated as I would have liked…It's strictly not a generic criticism of other skill types!

I use the term orchestra conductor deliberately because leading and closing a big deal requires that you know where you want to go and how to get there, but now you have to take every team member with you, including the Board, to achieve the desired result. Any one failure in the team performance can bring the whole deal down. You need to have a mindset that is akin to a political broker whereby you lead any discussion that has 'broken down' with the appropriate colleagues e.g. Legal, Technical, H.R.

During the final negotiations, it's crucially important that as each item is tabled and agreed, say for example price, that you formally minute that it's 'signed off' and there's no going back, otherwise you will find yourself in interminable loops. This is quite possible, unless you follow this advice, where the Legal teams are concerned. These people and their function are absolutely crucial to protecting you and your company's interests, however in my experience it doesn't take much for them to become overzealous on points of principle and for a contract term or condition negotiation to melt down into a professional 'deadlock' and never ending stalling scenarios between negotiating parties. It's key that you have the Executive Sponsor for your bid lined up with your client's Executive Sponsor, so if a final escalation is required for a decision on a term, then it can be triggered.

One extended (from a negotiation timescale perspective) deal I ran, where this unwanted scenario developed, necessitated me insisting that my COO and our Legal rep fly to Aberdeen in Scotland with me to close a deal where the customer's corresponding COO was so frustrated with the process and lack of progress that he offered both sides Legal teams his room to work in and told them not to come out until they had a resolution on disputed Terms &

Conditions! This was one of the world's largest oil companies. I got the deal and it was a groundbreaking project for the company at the time which led to many more reference deals.

Let's now move on to look at how you keep the closing phase in synchronisation between internal and external activities.

I mentioned above that 'synchronising' the deal was important so let me explain why in more detail.

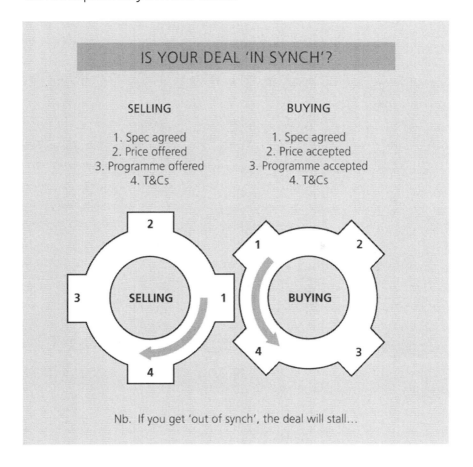

IS YOUR DEAL 'IN SYNCH'?

SELLING

1. Spec agreed
2. Price offered
3. Programme offered
4. T&Cs

BUYING

1. Spec agreed
2. Price accepted
3. Programme accepted
4. T&Cs

Nb. If you get 'out of synch', the deal will stall...

For simplicity sake (because sometimes there are a lot more), let's say there are four key phases to the closure post presentation; Agreeing the Spec, Agreeing the Price, Agreeing the Project Plan and, finally, the T&Cs.

If in the diagram the gears aren't meshed and the client wants to finalise the contract T&Cs before agreeing the price and your lawyers are insisting the opposite, then just like a broken or jammed car gearbox, the deal will stall until you broker a way out of it. Make sure you have agreed the steps with the client precisely and that once each is done, there is no going back.

"Fine," you say. "Wouldn't life be wonderful if all deals ran as smoothly as this?" But of course they don't, even with the best planning on the planet, so what gets in the way?

Differences of opinion on key items and the need to clarify them via negotiation not done upfront in the discovery phase pre-proposal is the usual one. So how do we handle these?

Negotiations

According to the dictionary, the definition of negotiation is 'to confer for the purpose of mutual arrangement or agreement'.

The important word in that statement for me is 'mutual' because if you don't get a mutually satisfying agreement, the client will feel aggrieved and motivated at some point in the future to 'restore the balance' as they see it. This is a counter productive psychological atmosphere in which to kick off a new project, so please avoid this scenario developing at all costs.

In order to get mutual satisfaction then, there has to be genuine positive intent to arrive at an agreeable bargain on a number of issues which are outstanding, whether they are technical, financial, legal or some complex blend of these. The amount of time you spend negotiating is in direct proportion to the amount of time you didn't get clarity during the discovery phase, well before you put your proposal and presentation together! As Mahan Khalsa quotes, "good negotiation won't compensate for bad consulting!"

So, as with the other steps, a good negotiation is a mix of optimising process and knowledge wrapped with good interpersonal technique based on NLP.

We will now look at;

• A good process

• Acquiring leveragable knowledge

• Interpersonal styles

Process

There are many training courses around the world on negotiation and no doubt hundreds of books, because the subject is so critical to a company's profitability and risk profile. One of the better ones I have attended was run by the Huthwaite Research Group, who specialise in a range of useful courses analogous to the material in this book and others. Just as a reminder, the USP of this book is that it integrates for the first time parts of many of the separate training techniques available into one seamless process in an eclectic fashion, together with my own ideas, techniques and processes.

Huthwaite recommend thinking about a number of important elements;

- Our objective

- Our fallback position

- A list of negotiable issues

- The prioritisation of these issues for you and the client (they will be different)

- The limits, best, target and worst for each issue

- An assumption of the client's target for each

- Cost of concessions

Again, as with Miller & Heiman's *Strategic Selling*, this whole process should not be undertaken lightly, say for example for a loosely qualified deal, as they take a long time to develop and the opportunity cost is high, so as above, try and sort out as much as possible before you get to this point to avoid protracted negotiations, or worse, ones that breakdown when you are very close to winning…

Once you have this framework of data composed, you now need to start to find information and knowledge that allows you to know when you should hold your ground and when you should give way.

Leverageable Information

The idea of leverageable information is that it supports you in any 'position' you may adopt and gives you negotiating power to use intelligently and sensitively. You do not use it to bludgeon your opponent into submission…remember the mutuality piece?

Types of leverageable information include;

Price; Has the price you have offered been thoroughly evaluated in terms of the value you will bring? In other words, if you have a strong ROI built into your proposal, and in particular if it's less than one year, then you must really make the client justify any price reduction requests.

T&Cs; Never give away or modify conditions in the contract that expose your company to risk that isn't covered in any contingency built into your price, particularly in fixed price contracts e.g. there is never usually a reason to agree to consequential loss or unlimited liquidated damages, but I have seen both accepted by desperate companies. If these type of things get asked for, ask the client which suppliers have conceded to them before and what is their justification now?

Timescales; If a client wants a shorter timescale, you need to be armed with reference case studies showing why you have based your estimates the way you have and that it is in their best interest i.e. for quality reasons, to stick to goals that are S.M.A.R.T based i.e. Specific, Measurable, Achievable, Realistic and Timely. It's expected that the client will want you to be aggressive with time, but it's in both parties' interest to have a successful and referenceable working project at the end of it. A serious point here though is that you must work with your bid manager very closely to make really sure that whoever has put your internal estimates together has done it with a view to selling something and not just having a 'comfortable' project.

On many occasions I have seen and been subsequently embarrassed in front of client, when a well-meaning technical person has tried to justify ridiculous 'contingency' estimates to no avail. If possible, put the estimating and potential delivery team on bonuses for winning and delivering 'on time and to budget'. Extra credit and reward should not just be for sales folks…

So these short examples are just that, but hopefully insightful enough for you to assemble your own key items ahead of any negotiation.

Now I would like to look at interpersonal style.

Interpersonal style

What I mean by this is the way that you and your bid team deliberately choose your attitude and communication style prior to the negotiation. Remembering the Enneagram. Again, it's a good idea to try and 'second-guess' whether the people you are going to negotiate with are from a heart, head or gut space. This will give you an insight as to how you might match and mirror to get rapport and use eye movements to detect what they are thinking and when. One eye movement to be very aware of is the 'visual construct' or when they look up to their right (your left as you look at them, if they are a right handed person), if it's pronounced and lengthy then it's likely they are 'making something up'…beware.

Apart from thinking through how you are going to get maximum rapport and therefore increased likelihood of a mutually satisfying outcome, it's also useful to prepare for hard negotiations by following Keith Eades' advice in his book *The New Solution Selling*. In it, he talks about three key mantras that are;

1. Be prepared and have valid arguments to defend at least four rounds of squeezing by buyers.

2. Don't give anything without getting something in return.

3. Be willing to walk away.

This last point has become more and more discussed in the recent avant-garde books on selling. It's a powerful technique and one that takes courage to use. Your mindset has to be one where you have imagined that you are already over quota and don't need this business to do your target…even if you do. It does, however, re-qualify your position and if you play this card, it's critical that you watch the buyer's facial expression. Very few can hide alarm as well as a poker player if they need what you are offering.

So having created your list of negotiable items as recommended previously, you now need to have in your head which ones you must hold onto at your 'Target' levels and which ones you can relax a little on to show flexibility. In any debate, heated or otherwise, keep calm, cool and collected and give things away in very small increments and only after being asked or 'squeezed' many times.

If you do find yourself in a rare position of 'deadlock', which does sometimes happen with the Legal elements, than you must have mutually pre-agreed escalation route that brings together senior final arbiters to resolve. You might want to even architect such a scenario to establish a good reason for your Exec 'C' Level person to meet theirs and get the deal closed there and then!

As stated previously, more than 60% of all communication between two parties or more is Non-Verbal (NVC) i.e. its body language.

If you are running a big deal, it's likely the client will be fielding a professional buying team of some sorts and in lots of cases an external Legal team. I know of one deal where a client, we estimated at the time, must have spent £750k with external lawyers on a £7.5m deal. Of course, lawyers on both sides are important, but well-paid managers are paid to do just what the title infers, manage risk, and not abdicate every call on a Term or Condition to advisers.

The point I'm making is that you need to prepare yourself and, as importantly, anyone who will be interfacing with the client on your team, with 'how we are going to play this deal with whom' type coaching well in advance of any negotiation session, otherwise you will be cannon fodder in the face of their buying team. So on your team you need a minimum cast of characters who will 'play' the following roles. (I use the word 'guy' here in a generic sense, not a gender one)

- 'Lead Guy'

- 'Tough Guy'

- 'Techie(s)'

- 'Well Briefed Lawyer'

- 'C' Level escalation person

The Lead Guy has to be you, the salesperson, because post-sale, if successful, you will need to nurture and grow this relationship and whatever you do or say during negotiations needs not to impact that possibility. The client doesn't expect you to be a pussycat or a walkover in the negotiations, but there may be times when the scenario gets heated and a walk away card gets played. The 'Tough Guy', not you, needs to throw that on the table. It may be something like a firm 'NO' to a term the client really wants you to move on. So, by example, perhaps you may use your own CFO to politely but firmly refuse 90 day payment terms when your estimate has factored 30 days for good cash flow reasons.

The 'Techie(s)' are those who know all the functional ins and outs of the product or service you offer and are individuals who can be trusted to face off to a client. Do not make the mistake though of assuming these folks will not be sometimes unwittingly naïve in front of the client… because unless you take the time to brief them properly, the odds are they may say something you don't want them to. I distinctly remember one 'challenging individual', I really mean 'un-briefed technical colleague' (my fault!), stating at a final pitch for a large IT outsourcing deal that (despite him already signing the delivery team size off at an internal meeting in ink) that subsequently he thought it 'might' need more people than he originally anticipated. This one simple comment severely dented our hard earned credibility with the client. It was only an assumption, not a fact, and upon investigation turned out to be incorrect. We didn't lose that deal, but we nearly did and the bid costs at that point were at £80k. So the message here for interpersonal styles is choose your bid team well and take the time to personally brief them ultra tightly on what they can and can't say, and to who.

The 'Well Briefed Lawyer' is another essential investment. What you need to get sorted and agreed with your own Executive Sponsor is the degree of risk associated with certain terms and conditions and how much you are willing to move, if at all, on the ones causing concern for the client. Do not let the lawyers dominate this, as there is a natural tendency for them to go for 'least-risk' scenarios every time, when in fact it's your company's job to manage risk and you hopefully have funds in the deal to cover such eventualities.

We have just mentioned the C Level Exec Sponsor and it's that individual's role to be the final arbiter on intransigent points that you and the customers team can't resolve. If you do play this card, only do it under the following terms. Stipulate to the client: "If I field my CXO and ask them to meet your CXO, it's only on the basis that there is mutual positive intent for this to be the final negotiation session and the meeting doesn't end until we have closure on all points."

This sounds tough but you need to be at this point, and when I and other sales professionals I know have requested such things, the negotiations have gone on until the wee hours of the morning. In one classic example, an amusing point arose when a software supplier to my organisation hadn't anticipated the possibility of this scenario and ended up booking into hotels and asking my PA to go out and buy fresh shirts, shorts and socks for the next day's activities! That deal was closed at 3am in the morning...

Getting it signed…

Now that you've done all this hard work on negotiations and have got all your outstanding points agreed, it's time to maintain the momentum and get the deal signed. There is, in my experience, a kind of weird hiatus that can kick in at this moment in time and, despite all good intentions from both parties, the energy dives on both sides and frustration can occur whilst you wait for them to process some signed paperwork.

As a motor sports fan, I want to paint an analogy which I hope will stick in your mind and prevent you from losing any deal at the finishing line. Essentially, the metaphor for where you are in the deal is that you are in the lead entering the last corner of what was a really tough Grand Prix and because you can see in your mirrors and you have heard from the pits over the radio that your competitor is at least 20 seconds behind, you believe you can switch off the motor and cruise over the line and victory will be yours… Never ever do this in a race car or in a business deal. You must keep your foot planted on that throttle until the chequered flag (signature on contract) has dropped over your car. You haven't won anything, either race or your contract, until this happens, so how do you get it done? Well really it's the last vital part of your closing 'project plan' that I referred to. Don't just have 'customer signs deal' as a line item on the plan. Have 'customer signs deal like this…' in precise detail with all the dates and people mapped out. I wish I had been paid a couple of grand for the number of times I have bailed out ailing sales folks at this point in the deal because I would be a lot richer! The sorts of things you need to know and have covered are;

- Who are the people who sign this deal and in what order? E.g. COO, then CFO , then CEO?

- Are they teed up to do it?

- Do you know for sure none of these people are about to go on holiday or in hospital! (Believe me it happens all the time and they don't care if the deal slips over your quarter or year end!)

- Can you orchestrate being allowed to 'walk' the contract around their office to meet the C Level signatories with your internal customer sponsor? This is a great tactic and one that I encouraged a sales person in my team to do one Christmas and he got the final CEO's signature on Christmas Eve, one hour before they left for their office party!

- Finally, if your competition are aggrieved at hearing they are losing, the more aggressive ones will be trying to occupy the diaries of your signatories trying to spoil your chances and get themselves back on table, so it's essential that you are filling your client's diaries, not them…

Keeping

Stage 4: Keeping the client satisfied

Some sales organisations advocate that once a piece of new business is done that the deal should be transferred from the new business ('Hunter type') sales person to someone more suited to relationship enhancement commonly known as an Account Manager/Director ('Farmer type'). Whilst I support this to an extent, I would strongly recommend a phased handover extended over some considerable months with careful monitoring of the client's reaction. Prior to any commercial handovers though, is a very important step, one that many organisations miss out and if it is, can cause untold damage to the newly sold project. This crucial step is the 'Sales to Product or Project Delivery handover'.

It is assumed that both delivery and sales work hand in hand to develop any solution offered, but what frequently happens is that the technical people who worked on the deal may well, by now, have gone off to another project whilst the deal was in its closing phase, which can of course take months. What the client doesn't understand is that your own organisation needs to maintain its people utilisation ratios and cannot always guarantee fielding the people they met during the bid.

In order to negate any bad feeling, or worse, creating a 'who sold you this then!' scenario between the delivery organisation and the client, it's essential that two 'sales to delivery handover meetings' are held. The first one is purely internal to your company and should comprise of Sales informing Delivery of the following;

- The business case and the pain/gain being addressed by the solution.

- The solution components as sold.

- The timescale if it's fixed price and budget.

- The commercial pricing.

- The terms and conditions.

- The risks and assumed mitigations.

- Any 'lock-ins' like key personnel agreements.

There shouldn't be any surprises at this stage but frequently there are because different engineers/consultants being what they are, they may well have differing views on how things can be delivered. Any points like this must be resolved before any future client interaction and at your company's cost.

The second meeting is a re-run of the above but includes the client's project team and its objective is to gain upfront agreement that as far as all parties are concerned, at this juncture, there is no impediment to the project being delivered on-time and to budget. It's also an opportune moment to start some team building between your delivery team and the client's project team, so make sure some kind of social kick-off is wrapped around this event to facilitate that initial bonding. Again, as the key customer interface, it's down to you to make sure that this is a bonding exercise and not an event that deteriorates into an egotistic 'antler clashing' nightmare.

Choose something where there isn't much chance of vast quantities of alcohol being consumed and where there is an opportunity for your delivery team and the client's team to mix and get to know each other e.g. a sporting event, where you have mixed client/ customer teams competing against each other. Karting has always worked well for me. Whilst this is competitive, it isn't quite as aggressive as paintballing where I once accidentally shot a client in the rear end at a close distance, something that took him a while to forgive me for!

Once you have successfully completed the handover, it's important to maintain regular contact with the client, even if you as the new business sales person are handing over to an account manager. I advocate being party to the first project reviews to calibrate the customer's perspective on how things are going and if necessary being his conduit back into the senior levels of your own organisation.

It's also a good time to ask the client if you can produce a press release about the deal and its objectives. Normally they are supportive because they benefit as much as you from such publicity in their industry sector as innovators, as you do in yours. When collaboratively writing such a release, it's important to keep in mind what results everyone is looking for, so that when the project is finished you can revisit the initial release and use it as a basis for a Client Reference Case Study White Paper.

This is the most powerful piece of collateral you can have in your sales bag or on your website, and will seriously enhance your opportunities to win more business with your wider client base, either existing or target (known as 'Leveraging' which we will come to next).

Or, and this is where World Class Account Managers operate, to utilise in your current client's organisation by revisiting the Value Chain model you built, looking at the organisation chart and deciding where you would like your Coach to help to access other C Level execs (known as 'Expanding', which will be the final part of this integrated sales approach and the last part of the book).

Leveraging

Stage 5: Leveraging into the wider client base

Having discussed how to successfully sell and then handover a new project into either a new or existing client, it is now timely to look at how you and of course your sales team colleagues, should exploit this win in a wider context with other prospects.

Having developed the press release, based on sound business rationale and strategy, one tactic you can deploy which will put you on a different level straightaway is to decide which organisations and 'C Level' contacts you want to get access to discuss their receptivity to a similar solution. Clearly you want to maintain your initial client's confidentiality but as most organisations know it's not the raw solution that intrinsically makes a difference competitively, but it's how it's deployed and used that gives a competitive edge. These latter aspects should be kept confidential from other clients and you should of course stick well within the terms of any confidentiality agreements.

There are a number of ways you can deploy to generate new leads that amongst many are;

- Ask your existing C Level client to introduce you to their peer network in other companies who they think would benefit from a similar solution.

- Use your own C Level team to write to your target C Level contacts with a covering letter and the press release asking for a meeting to explore mutually beneficial possibilities.

- Put the press release on your website.

- Work with the client to produce a presentation that can be given by them or you at industry conferences.

This latter tactic worked tremendously well for me during the time that the pharmaceutical industry was investigating Computer Aided New Drug Applications (CANDA) in the mid 1990s at the behest of the FDA. In 18 months, we opened 12 new clients and established relationships that are benefiting that System Integrator today.

Once you have some initial leads, it's time to go back to the middle of the 'Finding' stage of the sales cycle that I've outlined so far and start some in-depth qualification. If the opportunity passes that analysis to your satisfaction, then you can move into the diagnosis phase described in 'Investigating'.

Clearly what you are looking to do from here on in is to build a high quality funnel of leads that you can jointly qualify with the prospects. If there is an opportunity to develop an industry specific solution because of some nuance you've found that's likely to be relevant to most companies in that sector, now is the time to start feeding that information back to your Product Development and R&D folks. Be careful though on predicting rapid industry wide take-up. There is much wisdom in Geoffrey Moores' books; *The Gorilla Game*, *Crossing the Chasm* and *Inside the Tornado*, where he discusses, at length, the impact of a hiatus in the timeline of the introduction and market acceptance of new products and services. Read these and make sure that your organisation has enough funds and ideas to withstand such a potential lag in market demand for any new product launched.

Contrarily, don't miss the gains to be made by being the 'First Mover' in a market. Establishing market share and becoming the 'industry' solution for very large companies e.g. SAP in the ERP IT solutions market during the 1990s, is a very strong and profitable place to be, although since then we have seen conglomerating organisations like Infor hold their ground against them. The message I have learnt from both 'in-field' experience and academic study to MBA level is that the stronger and better your value proposition is articulated and understood by the client base, the quicker the market will accept it and drag it across the 'chasm' that Moore describes. An easy to understand analogy is that, as I write this book, I am agonising over which DVD camcorder to buy to record our imminent Summer holiday. The reason I have delayed buying one so far, and to be honest still reticent now, is the bewildering array of emerging so-called 'standards' that these devices are built to in order to capture and store moving images by. This must be causing a 'chasm' in the DVD camcorder market, much to the chagrin of the Japanese manufacturers.

It's very important that as you win more and more clients that you deliberately develop a 'balanced' and resilient set of customers. Although it becomes almost irresistible due to the growth enhancing nature of the opportunity, very large deals that are much bigger than you've done before can become a monster to manage and can lose you a lot of negotiating power to the client if they know it. Also, if that client goes away and you've been heavily depending on the revenues, you are again exposed.

These considerations then should form part of your qualification i.e. 'Do we really want to have a deal/client this big in our portfolio?'

The following diagram is an attempt to graphically demonstrate this, whereby my suggestion is that the preferred model is where the exit of your largest client is potentially a painful scenario but not a business killing one…

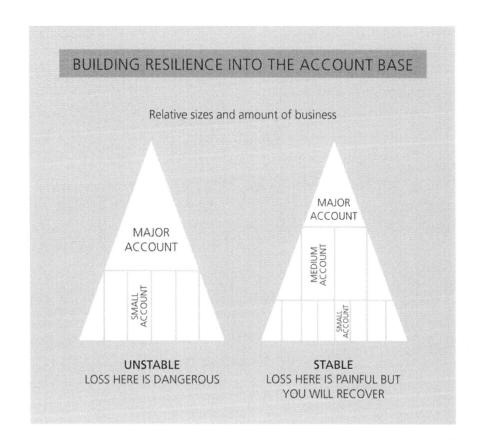

Expanding

Stage 6 Expanding back into the original customer

This stage really investigates going back to your original customer, after ensuring that all is well with the original deal and subsequent project, with a view to looking for more leads and opportunity. The concept is well known as 'increasing wallet share'.

Whether or not the client has a defined budget there will undoubtedly be other areas of their business where there will be issues (pain) and opportunities (gain) to derive additional value propositions from.

Mapping out your client's organisation using Porter's 'Value Chain Model', previously described and shown again here together with a comprehensive organisation chart, is the start point of this activity. Once you have these described in detail, ask your coach or Executive Sponsor of your original project to suggest who else in their business might be open to a discussion about their challenges. Once you have these names, ask your supporters to sponsor introductions and, suitably armed with a case study of your success so far with this client, start the 'Investigation' level discussions over again.

understand where the pain is, pure is to be able
to have valuable conversations

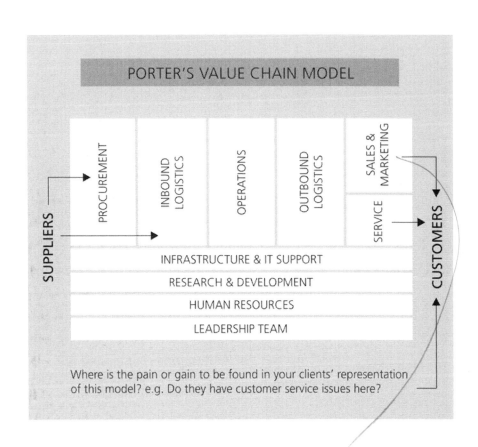

PORTER'S VALUE CHAIN MODEL

SUPPLIERS

PROCUREMENT

INBOUND LOGISTICS

OPERATIONS

OUTBOUND LOGISTICS

SALES & MARKETING

SERVICE

CUSTOMERS

INFRASTRUCTURE & IT SUPPORT

RESEARCH & DEVELOPMENT

HUMAN RESOURCES

LEADERSHIP TEAM

Where is the pain or gain to be found in your clients' representation of this model? e.g. Do they have customer service issues here?

ie Nick is inching himself here

Further expansion opportunities can be 'taken' to the client by pro-actively gathering intelligence from the 'eco-system' of suppliers that also operate in the client and with whom you must have a solid networking relationship. In my early days as a hardware salesman, I developed this model to enhance my opportunities by knowing exactly who else was selling into the client, be they software companies, Telcos, management consultants etc. Once you have garnered this information, you can start to populate the 'Selling Matrix' shown in the diagram below.

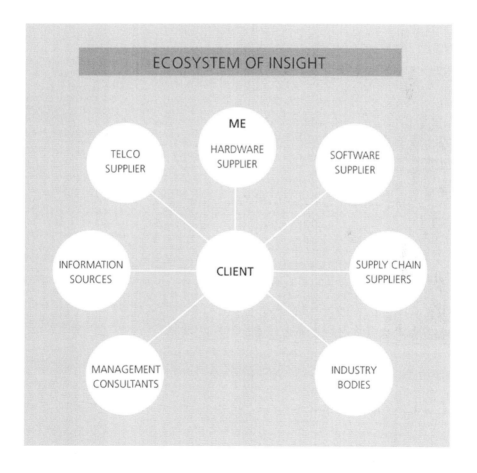

Utilising the 'Selling Matrix' to strategically plan your next pro-active campaign into the client is showing the highest levels of Account control and development, and is a fundamental part of 'Expanding' your market share.

By understanding where you are, where the competition are and what you don't know about the account, will drive your actions and appointment seeking campaigns.

Again, this also helps you in the qualification stages of an opportunity because you are now able to judge the likely competitor strength and their likely tactics, thus allowing you to decide with better information and insight whether you want to play or not!

I have used an example here from my career in IT so you need to substitute those offerings with your own as well as tune the client's functional areas to the relevant ones for you.

MATRIX SELLING

PRODUCTS OR SERVICES	INBOUND LOGISTICS	MANUFACTURING	OUTBOUND LOGISTICS	SALES AND MARKETNG	FINANCE	HR	R & D
DECISION SUPPORT	DK	O	DK	C	O	O	C
ERP	C	O	C	DK	O	O	NA
REALTIME	C	DK	C	NA	NA	NA	DK

CLIENT FUNCTIONAL AREAS

KEY
0 - OURS
C - COMPETITION
DK - DON'T KNOW
NA - NOT APPLICABLE

*"There may be some substitute for
hard facts, but if there is,
I have no idea what
it can be."*

J Paul Getty

Your Personal Performance

If you've managed to stay with the book this far, you are probably wondering what it takes as an individual to be successful in this game of high value complex deal selling.

On my website www.apexselling.com, there is a Self Analysis tool that you can use free of charge, which allows you to measure yourself against some 20 criteria. Once you have done this, you can think through your strengths, weakness, opportunities and threats for yourself as a salesperson and then reflect on the following two diagrams.

Having done the 'Self Analysis' on the site, where would you plot yourself on the 'Skill/Will' matrix on the next page? I'm hoping you haven't landed in 'Remove'?

More likely you will say either you don't know enough and therefore will seek some training, or you've reflected on just how motivated you are these days and whether you are happy doing what you're doing. If it's the former, talk to us to see if we can help.

If it's the latter, then we may be able to help there too but you need to get to the root of it because this environment does not reward apathy.

I developed this last model as part of thinking through for this book what are the optimum characteristics these days for a high performing and equally important, happy and motivated salesperson. Well in addition to the criteria on the site, you will be relieved to know that you don't have to be a rocket scientist, but as you would

SKILL/WILL MATRIX

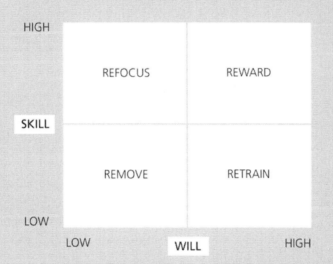

HIGH

SKILL

LOW

| | REFOCUS | REWARD |
| | REMOVE | RETRAIN |

LOW   WILL   HIGH

Source; Max Landberg; The Tao of Coaching 2nd Edition
(Profile Business 2003) page 55.

expect, a reasonable IQ is a pre-requisite for strategising your moves with colleagues and being creative with proposal content.

EQ, as most of you will know, is Emotional Quotient (not Erotic Quotient, as some comedian suggested to me recently!) and this is the ability to create rapport with others and maintain your emotional stability in times of great stress. A real life example is the scenario discussed in the foreword by my friend Geoff Bingley where we worked around the clock for two days to get a bid out together. The temptation to lose your temper over simple things when you haven't slept for two days can be enormous!

Finally, for me a function of success is encapsulated in the time honoured phrase, 'It's who you know that gets you on in life' and boy, is this true. So your Social Quotient (SQ) must be something you consciously maximise. Here's how it worked for me when I set up Apexselling Ltd in 2012.

Just 14 days after joining LinkedIn, I had circa 150 direct contacts, 30,000 second level contacts and 3,000,000 third level which immediately produced 5 C Level opportunities with companies I had never done business with....IQ x EQ x SQ = £

TRIANGLE OF COMPETENCE AND CREDIBILITY

EQ

ABILITY TO LEAD,
MANAGE, INSPIRE AND
CREATE RAPPORT
WITH OTHERS

IQ

RAW INTELLECT,
QUALIFICATIONS AND
ACCREDITATIONS

SQ

THE NUMBER OF PEOPLE YOU
KNOW WITH INFLUENCE

Importantly, I would like to leave you with some final thoughts regarding your self development. The whole reason for writing this book was to help you climb the steps of competence on the 'Learning Ladder'. You will recognise these steps from whatever you have attempted in the past professionally or personally, maybe in sports? Even when you feel you've reached Level 4 in selling 'high value and complex' deals, it's important to keep refreshing your skills. To that end, I hope this book becomes a resource you can dip into throughout your career.

WHY HAVE TRAINING FOR ANYTHING?

Because unless you are at Level 4 for any profession,
sport or art, you will not win...

LEVEL 4 - UNCONSCIOUS COMPETENCE

LEVEL 3 - CONSCIOUS COMPETENCE

LEVEL 2 - CONSCIOUS INCOMPETENCE

LEVEL 1 - UNCONSCIOUS INCOMPETENCE

"The Learning Ladder"

"Never give in, never give in, never; never; never; - in nothing, great or small, large or petty - never give in except to convictions of honour and good sense."

Winston Churchill

Conclusion

Hopefully by now, I have achieved my ambition with this book, which was to enlighten you to the benefits of having a well thought out professional campaign for any future large complex deals that you pursue.

As you will no doubt agree, if you have been in sales for a reasonable amount of time, selling is neither a science or an art, but an eclectic mix of the two and of course a dash of good old fashioned luck is always welcome. But, as one author titled his own sales book, 'Hope is not a Strategy'. You can't bet the farm on luck arriving either, so it's much better to have a well thought out and executable plan.

'Plan the work, work the plan!'

The best approach is to thoroughly think through, and define a process and set of accompanying actions that fit the way you work. You now have mine and it works.

I have given you the processes, thoughts, questions and actions to consider, which cover most of the angles and challenges you will face in this game, plus a whole reading list of other references to buy, research and read to add to your own portfolio.

If you need more help, contact me via www.apexselling.com.

Meanwhile, keep your activities honest, ethical, professional and well planned and you will in time, coupled with a great deal of dogged persistence and tenacity become very successful and build a fabulous reputation for your company and yourself.

My favourite all-time saying is Dale Carnegie's "Persistence is to the character of man as carbon is to steel", and this is the one outstanding attribute that you will need to succeed...

We didn't go into the personal attributes needed to win and survive in this game, (maybe that's my next book!) but in my view you need to be a motivated, ambitious, intelligent, tenacious (persistent), focused, personable, assertive team player with a good sense of humour and a 'never say die' attitude. If you have these and can couple them with the content of this book, then you are well on your way to financial freedom and contentment in life!

A final thought from the writer Somerset Maugham;

"If you don't change your beliefs, your life will be this way forever. Is that good news?"

References

Eades, Keith M. (2003), *The New Solution Selling: The Revolutionary Sales Process That is Changing the Way People Sell*, 2nd edition, McGraw-Hill Professional

Hanan M. (1987), *Consultative Selling: The Hanan Formula for High-Margin Sales at High Levels*, third edition, Amacom Books

Johnson, Kerry (1994), *Selling with NLP: Revolutionary New Techniques That Will Double Your Sales Volume*, Nicholas Brealey Publishing

Khalsa, Mahan, and Illig, Randy (1999), *Let's Get Real and Let's Not Play: The Demise of 20th Century Selling & the Advent of Helping Clients Succeed*, FranklinCovey Company Inc., an imprint of Penguin Group (USA) Inc.

Maisters, David H. (1997), *Managing the Professional Service Firm*, Simon & Schuster

Miller, Robert and Heiman, Stephen (1987), *Strategic Selling: The Unique Sales System Proven Successful by America's Best Companies*, Miller-Heiman, Inc

Moore, Geoffrey A. (1998), *Crossing the Chasm: Marketing and Selling Technology Products to Mainstream Customers*, second edition, Capstone Publishing Limited

Oulton, Nicholas B. (2005), *Killer Presentations: Power to the Imagination to Visualise Your Point - with PowerPoint*, How To Books Ltd

Peoples, David (1993), *Selling to the Top: David Peoples' Executive Selling Skills*, John Wiley & Sons

Porter, Michael E. (1985), *Competitive Advantage*, New York: Free Press

Riso, Don Richard and Hudson, R. (1999), *The Wisdom of the Enneagram: Complete Guide to Psychological and Spiritual Growth for the Nine Personality Types*, Bantam USA

Thull, Jeff (2004), *Mastering the Complex Sale: How to Compete and Win When the Stakes are High!*, John Wiley & Sons

Turner, Diane and Greco, Thelma (2001), *The Personality Compass: A New Way to Understand People*, second edition, Thorsons

Glossary

C or CXO Level; Any Chief Level person e.g. Chief Executive Officer (CEO).

Column Fodder; The list that sophisticated buyers use whereby they evaluate a raft of vendors and score them against a predetermined set of criteria. The 'columns' represent A to wherever e.g. G, equal to the number of bidders. If you are not in Column A, then you are in B onwards, and just making up the numbers.

DMU; Decision Making Unit, which in effect is the set of people that are involved in evaluating your bid from the client's side which normally includes a C Level person.

Enneagram; A personality typing tool, the aim of which is to enhance interpersonal communication by the recognition and adaptation to personal diversity, based on nine types of people.

Footprint; The conceptual area or amount of market share you occupy in the client's annual spend, otherwise known as 'wallet share'.

NLP; Neuro Linguistic Programming, a concept which has been around for some over 20 years and is a self development tool which in essence says you are in charge of what goes in your mind and how you feel about it. Furthermore, how you relate to others and the quality of that interaction is under your influence.